HEIRLOOM HERBS

HEIRLOOM HERBS

Using Old-Fashioned Herbs in Gardens, Recipes, and Decorations

MARY FORSELL

Photographs by
TONY CENICOLA

Foreword by
ROSEMARY VEREY

VILLARD BOOKS
NEW YORK 1990

A Running Heads Book

Copyright © 1990 by Running Heads Incorporated. Photographs © Tony Cenicola.

All rights reserved under International Pan-American Copyright Conventions. Published in the United States by Villard Books, a division of Random House, Inc., New York, and simultaneously in Canada by Random House of Canada Limited, Toronto.

Library of Congress Cataloging-in-Publication Data
Forsell, Mary.
    Heirloom herbs : using old-fashioned herbs in gardens, recipes, and decorations / by Mary Forsell ; photographs by Tony Cenicola.
      p.   cm.
    ISBN 0-394-58336-1 : $29.95
    1. Herbs—Heirloom varieties. 2. Herb gardening. I. Cenicola, Tony. II. Title.
    SB351.H5F6   1991
    635′.7—dc20   90-50195
                                       CIP

HEIRLOOM HERBS
was conceived and produced by Running Heads Incorporated
55 West 21st Street
New York, NY 10010

Editor: Charles de Kay
Designer: Jack Tom
Managing Editor: Lindsey Crittenden
Production Manager: Linda Winters

Typeset by David E. Seham Associates, Inc.
Color separations by Hong Kong Scanner Craft Company, Ltd.
Printed and bound in Singapore by Times Offset Pte Ltd.

10 9 8 7 6 5 4 3 2 1

A number of herbal medicinal practices are described in this book. In many cases the history of the usages of herbs is given; in other cases contemporary medicinal usages are addressed. Such information is not intended as a recommendation of any medicinal practice, and ailments should always be taken to your physician or herbalist. A few herbal healing recipes are provided in the final chapter of this book, and these should prove helpful in alleviating minor ailments and must be administered as described. The author and publisher cannot assume responsibility for adverse reactions to herbs.

    Bear in mind, too, that it is illegal in the United States and Europe to dig up certain wild plants. Unless you are positive about the identity of a plant, do not harvest it from the wild. Consult region-specific field guides, some of which are listed in the Bibliography, and local authorities about plant identities.

DEDICATION

For all the herb cultivators, cooks, and crafters who freely shared their secrets

ACKNOWLEDGMENTS

It's wonderful to have people to call upon when you need advice, encouragement, and information. For this book, Running Heads editor Charles de Kay provided just these qualities with his easygoing yet motivational style. At Villard Books, editor Alison Acker generated ongoing enthusiasm while reserving astute, scholarly, and witty commentary for when it was most needed—and appreciated. Running Heads' Linda Greer was indispensable—a culinary expert, mathematician, and good friend all in one person. Also at Running Heads, Marta Hallett, Ellen Milionis, Lindsey Crittenden, Linda Winters, Sarah Kirshner, and Ellie Watson laid the groundwork for and oversaw the project, each making her own distinctive contribution. Jack Tom produced a gorgeous design, with Beth Collette's cheerful assistance. Thanks to Elizabeth Keihm at M. M. Fenner Company, ABC Antiques, and Dean & Deluca for help in styling a beautiful jacket photograph.

A number of personal acquaintances also shared their expertise. Naomi Black and Florence Kass offered culinary advice; Francine Lerner had medicinal insights; Arthur Nersesian scoured bookshelves for unusual sources; and Lynn Forsell helped me get in touch with regional sources.

Holly Shimizu of the U.S. Botanic Garden; Susan Moody at the Cloisters in New York; Betty Rea of McLean, Virginia; and Nicolas Ekstrom of the New York Horticultural Society each contributed advice and resources and receive grateful acknowledgment. In New York State, thanks go to Pat Reppert of Shale Hill Farm in Saugerties; Anne and Larry Salomon of Tweefontein Herb Farm in New Paltz; Ujjala

Schwartz of Ujjala's Bed and Breakfast, New Paltz; Dora Gerber of Swissette Herb Farm in Salisbury Mills; Pam Montgomery of Green Terrestrial in Milton; herbalist Susun Weed of Woodstock; Wendy, Michael, Sophie, and Max London of Rock Hill Bakehouse in Greenwich; and the Shaker Museum staff in Old Chatham.

In Manhattan, craftswoman Connie Wolfe; the landscape design firm of Cahill & Gardner Associates; and Morris-Jumel Mansion staff

also provided their unique input. In New Jersey, Cyrus and Louise Hyde of Well-Sweep Herb Farm were a godsend; and the Blew family near Flemington were as cheerfully cooperative as their sunflowers.

In England, a number of gardeners, horticultural experts, and chefs spent time with us. Each of these people contributed valuable information to this book: Lt. Col. D. G. Carpenter, administrator of the National Gardens Scheme; Leith's Restaurant, London; Margaret Moore, Little Herbs, Hertfordshire; Douglas McCord and David Beaumont, Hatfield House, Hertfordshire; Cannizaro House, London; Iden Croft Herbs, Kent, and owner Rosemary Titterington; Culpeper Ltd., London; Harrods, London, and Gareth Ballance; Chelsea Physic Garden, London, and director Donald Duncan; Tradescant Garden at the Museum of Garden History, London, and chairman Rosemary Nicholson; Paul Marsh of London; Andy Hart and the R. H. S. Garden at Wisley, Surrey; Capel Manor and director Robert Latchfield, Hertfordshire; Sandra French of Leed's Castle, Kent, and Chris Dee; Steve Gambol, Douglas Goodyear, Timothy Walker, Oxford University Botanic Gardens; the staff of Rothay Manor, Cumbria; Acorn Bank and gardener Christopher Braithwaite; Sellett Hall Herbs, Lancashire, and owner Judith Gray; and Fleur and Alan Marsh, Eyhorne Manor, Kent.

In Scotland, thank you to Prestonfield House, Edinburgh; R. Crawford and the Edinburgh Botanic Garden; Dr. David Stuart, Plants from the Past, Dunbar; Robin St Clair-Ford of the Scottish Gardens Scheme; Dr. Howden of the Late Victorian Pharmacy, Edinburgh; the Reids of Dunbar; and Hazel Herschell of the Scottish Tartans Museum.

In Sweden and Denmark, any language barrier was easily bridged by herbs. Thanks go to Pernilla Fredricksson, formerly of Skåne, Sweden, but now an itinerant sometimes-herbalist; Lars Björk of the Department of Pharmacology at the Royal Institute of Technology/Biomedical Centre of Uppsala University; Tomas Grunberg, herb consultant of Stockholm; Djurgärdsbrunns Wärdshus in Stockholm; Stallmästaregården and Richard Magnusson of Stockholm; Eva Vollner, director of Linnaeus' Garden and Museum in Uppsala; Count Thord Bond of Bosjökloster, Skåne; Visingsö herb garden; Tage Anderson, plant craftsman of Copenhagen, Denmark; St. Gertrude's Kloster, Copenhagen, Denmark; and, with very special thanks, Eva Falck of Tirup's Örtagård, Staffanstorp, Skåne, Sweden.

CONTENTS

FOREWORD

Herbs have long been a universal pleasure. All countries have their favorites, chosen to suit their climate and their palette. In the scheme of things herbs are between vegetables and flowers. They may not have the practical, prosaic usefulness of vegetables—although anyone who has enlivened a summer soup or a dish of pasta or potatoes with a handful of freshly picked mint or tarragon will realize their culinary value—but they take their place in the flower border in a way that vegetables do not, and in the vegetable garden they make a beautiful edging to the paths. The flowers of herbs have a modest charm of their own, although there is nothing shy about the breathtaking beauty of a mass of poppies, alliums, or lavender in full bloom. And the foliage of herbs is among the most rewarding of any plant. I cannot imagine my garden without variegated thymes, purple-leaved clover and sage, turquoise-blue rue and, perhaps my favorite, coppery-bronze fennel with its tall feathery outline that complements so many herbaceous flowers and shrubs.

Apart from the qualities of herbs as individuals, a herb plot is one of the most attractive small-scale gardens to create and enjoy. Do this in ordered patterns (maybe outlined in box) or planted with overflowing luxuriance. A herb garden needs no window dressing from other brilliant flowers—herb foliage makes a varied and harmonious tapestry of leaves, and its gentle flowers are a bonus. Above all, of course, there are the scents—crushed in your fingers they linger, and as you walk by they waft towards you in a tantalising medley.

A herb garden can be like a dolls' house—perfection in miniature. Just look at the design of a herb garden and you are looking into the mind and personality of its creator. My own herb garden is formal, patterned in box, rather like a pair of elongated tongs scissoring up towards the kitchen door. If the rest of my garden were taken from me, I would be content to be left with my herb garden. In winter the clipped box that divides it into diamonds stands out architecturally, and in summer the compartments overflow with sage, chamomile, parsley, and hyssop.

With all these attractions, I must not forget a major attribute of herbs—their medicinal qualities. Even these are not just pharmaceutical: when you drink an infusion of mint or chamomile leaves, you are doing something far more rewarding than visiting the chemist's shop; you are using a cure stretching back over continents and civilizations, attended by a wealth of history, folklore, and magic.

Herbs cast a permanent spell on anyone who uses them. For me, they are part of my everyday life. They scent my room, make me sleep more soundly, and can elevate an ordinary meal to a banquet. Perhaps the greatest virtue of this book is that it explores the mystery of herbs—their history, growing, and use so fully and sensitively— and leaves their magic intact.

Rosemary Verey
Barnsley House
Gloucestershire, England

THE
HISTORY
OF HERB
GARDENS

ANCIENT HERBALISM

Magical, flavorful, and hauntingly fragrant, herbs are living links with the past. The herbs we use each day are relatives of the basils, rosemary, thymes, and parsleys known to ancient peoples. They touch on so many aspects of our lives that they have become some of the most treasured of garden plants.

Long before the first days of recorded history, these unassuming plants were essential to human existence. The earliest evidence of herb consumption is recorded in the pollen grains of an ancient relative of wild marjoram. The ages-old pollen was discovered in dwelling caves that date from sixty thousand years ago. Even before they could write, people used herbs, consuming them instinctively, guided by their distinctive flavors and their usefulness in times of sickness. They harvested sweet-smelling thymes, lavender, and rosemary from rocky mountainsides; picked tansy from weedy meadows, elecampane from woodland clearings; and they carried aromatic armfuls of others from marshes and forests. It was among these first humble herb gatherers that botany and medicine began. Neanderthal people—who lived in Europe, Asia, and northern Africa fifty to one hundred thousand years ago—placed such great importance on plants that they buried their dead covered with wildflowers.

The Cloisters in Manhattan recreates the mood of a medieval courtyard garden and contains plants cultivated by monks before 1520, opposite. A genuine antique, London's Chelsea Physic Garden pays homage to those who studied there, including the physician Sir Hans Sloane, right.

As civilizations developed and people began settling into communities, there was a natural impulse to cultivate those prized wild species nearer home. The wondrous merits of herbs were first recorded on paper beginning in the third millennium B.C. These early writings were the very first herbals, and for centuries monks and botanists continued to write descriptive tomes outlining the healing properties of various

plants. Most herbs were first singled out for their medicinal qualities, rather than for the culinary merits that we value nowadays.

A Sumerian clay tablet from 3000 B.C. gives formulas for mixing such herbs as thyme and mustard with water, wine, and milk to create healing poultices and salves. The first Chinese herbal, *Pen-ts'ao Kang-mu,* is said to date from the third millennium B.C. and is attributed to Shen Nong, who may or may not have been an emperor. In any case, Shen Nong had a green thumb, for the author of *Pen-ts'ao Kang-mu* reports extensive experiments with plants and records many preparations he invented for

healing. Halfway around the world, about a thousand years later, a scribe in Egypt was fastidiously listing on papyrus medical, cosmetic, and household usages of herbs. We learn that the somewhat sybaritic Egyptians used henbane as a sedative and aloe to ease intestinal discomforts. Anyone rich enough to have a top-notch grave could ensure that his or her pyramid workers who were affected by scurvy received plenty of the *Allium* species plants (garlic and onions), which would restore their health—and return them to work—quickly. Anise and marjoram were used for embalming, and, among other splendors, living herb plants were entombed with the dead.

Herbs are mentioned in the Old Testament, which is thought to date from 1200 B.C. Anise, cumin, mint, lavender, and others are cited, as well as "bitter herbs," which are symbolized today in the horseradish and cos lettuce eaten during the Jewish seder of Passover. In ancient Greece, herbs were an essential part of everyday life.

Hippocrates, who lived from 460 to 370 B.C., based his medical treatments on objective observation and stressed proper diet and hygiene as cures. He was born on the Greek island of Cos and did much of his scientific work there. Hippocrates is reputed to have assembled a list of several hundred herbs with healing powers, although historians now believe that this list might have been the work of other doctors who were following in the Hippocratic tradition.

Perhaps the most monumental and important early work on herbs is Dioscorides's *De Materia Medica* of A.D. 77. *De Materia Medica* recorded cures involving about six hundred plants, and it remained the principal source of information for Western physicians until the sixteenth century, when its preeminent position was threatened by the publication of John Gerard's much-thumbed-through *The Herball.* Dioscorides's work was actively used by some pharmacists as a reference until the eighteenth century. Later, Marcus Aurelius's doctor, Galen, who lived from A.D. 130 to 200, contributed his findings on medicinal plants and even detailed a potion for what sounds very much like cold cream.

The ancient Greeks used herbs for more than medicine. Athletes celebrated their victories with crowns of bay and parsley, the goddess Aphrodite was worshiped with roses, and rosemary garlands were as commonplace at festivals as balloons are at modern-day parades. For their scent violets were strewn on floors of public buildings, and mint was used for fragrant baths and as a flavoring for sauces. Although there were private Greek gardens, the majority of herbs were cultivated outside the cities in large, orderly plots that supplied the city markets with herbs and flowers for garlands, ceremonies, and medicine.

The Romans, influenced by the Greeks in the uses of herbs, created a style of gardening all their own. They built private enclosed courtyard gardens featuring symmetrically arranged beds and boxwood topiary. The statesman Pliny the Elder recorded that the wealthiest citizens created elaborate courtyard gardens—not only in their city gardens but also at their private villas in the country. Even the middle class enjoyed a gardening tradition. They brought water in via aqueducts and made their small gardens seem larger by painting murals of broad vistas blooming with trees, flowers, and shrubs. Plantings included such herbal flowers as roses, violets, and irises and traditional cooking herbs, such as rosemary, parsley, coriander, and dill.

Much as in Grecian culture, herbs infused every possible aspect of Roman life. Citizens languished in herbally scented baths and afterward fell fast asleep on plump pillows stuffed with rose petals. They concocted delicately flavored herbal sauces to consume at their feasts—and afterward a satisfied statesman might facilitate digestion with fennel and senna. Even today in many Italian and Italian-American households, chunks of fresh Florence fennel bulbs are placed on the table after a meal.

In Rome, herbs such as carnations and

violets were prized for the delicate flavor they brought to wines and liqueurs. But herbs were also used for murderous purposes by spurned lovers, who avenged their malefactors with belladonna, or deadly nightshade.

THE MIDDLE AGES

In the time of the Holy Roman Empire, during Charlemagne's rule in the ninth century, the emperor made a decree stating which plants he wanted grown in gardens throughout his empire. Many herbs, including roses, made the list. After Charlemagne's empire dissolved in the late

Bosjökloster, an ancient convent in Sweden, above, features a small yet varied herb garden. At Hatfield House in England, right, lemon verbena, santolina, and lavenders line a stairway. A continent away in the United States, container herbs flourish in a sunny courtyard at the Cloisters, opposite.

ninth century, a period of raiding and warring commenced in Europe. The monarchal structure broke down, and feudalism was introduced. Noblemen erected lavish castles for themselves and built hovels for their subjects. These stratified communities were then sealed against raiding enemies by walls and moats with herb gardens both inside and out. Garden plots containing herbs used both to mask the taste of food that hadn't been refrigerated and for medicinal purposes were essential to these communities.

From this tradition of the walled community arose the monastic garden. Monasteries became the stronghold of knowledge and learning for all of Europe. Herbs were grown abundantly in the monasteries, and their uses were recorded in herbals. Washing their hands of the barbarism of the day, the monks created wholly self-reliant societies. At their hermitages they invented their own system of herb gardening. Medicinal herbs were found in the physic garden, vegetable and cooking herbs in the kitchen garden, and flowering herbs in the ornamental beds, which supplied fresh blossoms to decorate the church for holy days.

By the late Middle Ages wars had become less of a threat. The monks opened their doors to the outside world and took on commercial ventures. To raise money, they dispensed medicinal herbs to the public and actually ran infirmaries. Monasteries also became travelers' inns, offering overnight accommodation. The monks catered to their tired guests' whims, cooking up unusual and sumptuous dishes with herbs and serving aromatic herbal wines of their own creation. The monks gleaned much of their knowledge from the old herbals, transcribing and adding to their information. Pilgrims supplied them with information on herbal practices elsewhere and conveyed messages between monasteries, further disseminating herbal knowledge.

During the Crusades, in the years from the eleventh to the thirteenth centuries, there was an explosion in the range of plants grown in Europe. Crusaders brought unfamiliar plants back home with them, and many of these found their way into monastery gardens. Even with this rich influx of raw materials the monks of that era, while keeping earlier treatments in use, did not add many cures of their own. But their contributions to herbalism are significant since they kept many unusual herbs in cultivation while also developing new methods for raising them.

When selecting plants for their herb gardens, the monks were confronted with a serious problem. They had to choose from a vast range of native European herbs and the thousands more that had been introduced from foreign lands. To select the plants that would combat a wide range of illnesses, they were guided by the Doctrine of Signatures, which stated that a plant's appearance, in terms of both color and form, indicated how it should be used. This belief sprang up in countries as disparate as China and Sweden. It was thought that God invested every plant with a different way of serving humanity, and so every species could be used in some way. Plants with yellow flowers were thought good for curing jaundice; a plant with inflated parts would certainly be the cure for dropsy, an early name for edema; and a plant with a peculiar habit would inspire a related usage in medicine—for example, Saint John's wort "bleeds" red oil from its leaf glands; hence doctors used it to dress bleeding wounds. Owing to the persistent medicinal usage of some plants up to modern times, it would seem that coincidence and luck often resulted in a good match.

The infamous Black Death, which swept through Europe in the fourteenth century, placed even greater demands on the medicinal herb garden. The plague prompted the usage of such herbs as thyme, angelica root, burnet, and rue as tonics and preventatives. These herbs were used in successive centuries as other waves of the plague swept through Europe and Asia. Europeans desperate for herbal cures for the

plague paid exorbitant prices for exotic herbal remedies concocted by Arabic Muslims in Baghdad. In those days the Arabians controlled the drug and spice trade, and many Arab physicians had become highly learned in herbal medicine, drawing on Greco-Roman, Indian, Far Eastern, and Persian texts.

By the fifteenth century several millennia of herbal usage and folklore had resulted in a complex system of beliefs surrounding the magical powers of these plants. Herbs were thought not only to heal but also to protect by means of their mystical powers. Superstition surrounded a long list of herbs, and many unusual, ritualistic traditions were inspired by them. For example, in England, marjoram sprigs were placed near containers of milk to keep them from curdling; in Italy the condition of mugwort placed under the pillow of an ailing person was used as a means of foretelling the future; and such herbs as rue, elder, and dill kept about the house were thought to protect against evil spirits. Even if an herb could provide a cure, oftentimes it was a witch on whom the original trouble would be blamed. This period saw the rise of witch trials in Europe and Great Britain, which went on until the eighteenth century. Many charms—rituals involving herbs and often the repetition of a few magical phrases—had developed in different cultures, and anyone

caught practicing them gave a nervous citizenry grounds for accusations of witchcraft, even if the intended result of the charm had been merely to heal a wart. Thousands of people, particularly women, went on trial for, and more often than not were found guilty of, consorting with the dark forces.

Much of witches' magical power was said to be derived from herbs, especially those plucked on Midsummer Eve, June 23. In some countries this ancient pagan holiday became Christianized as St. John's Eve. In France it was long believed that herbs could protect a person from evil and ensure good health if they were gathered before dawn, while the person fasted on Midsummer Eve. One version of the Midsummer superstition required walking backward and incanting magic words while harvesting the herbs.

Botanomancy—divination through plants—grew out of this rich tradition. In northern Europe, particularly the Scandinavian countries, unmarried girls were taught that magical wildflowers plucked on Midsummer Eve and gathered into bouquets or wreaths would enable them to see their future bridegrooms in their dreams.

THE RENAISSANCE

By Tudor times in England the herb was firmly entrenched in secular daily life. Because the monasteries had been disbanded by Henry VIII, monks no longer studied or recorded the powers of herbs. Many commoners had already established their own herbal beds, though. The homes of the gentry boasted herb gardens of complicated design bordered by fragrant plants, and in those stately homes flowers were sometimes even dried in silver sand and used as food garnishes. Cottagers made room for herbs, too, in small plots of "pot-

A signpost at an upstate New York farm points the way to the herb garden, above. Across the Atlantic, herbs thrive in centuries-old settings: London's Chelsea Physic Garden, opposite above and below left, and the Linnaeus Garden in Uppsala, Sweden, opposite below right.

herbs" with which to add taste and color to simple meals. In his *Five Hundred Points of Good Husbandry,* of 1573, the widely read poet Thomas Tusser recommended a number of "necessarie herbes to growe in the garden for physick" as well as "stilling herbes" (for distilling), "strowing herbes" (strewing herbs to cover the floor), "herbes for the kitchen," "herbes for rootes for sallets and sauce," and herbs "to boile or to butter." His list included well over a hundred species.

The Tudor years also marked the onset of the herb-filled botanical and university garden. The design of this type of garden, often with checkerboard-patterned beds, was based on the monastic garden—which was fitting since these gardens succeeded the hermitages as centers of herbal learning. Because the universities often had medical

schools, too, medical botany became a discipline that could be practiced by close observation of the herbal bed. The first such university botanic garden in England was established at Oxford in 1621, complete with a nursery of "simples," that is, plants that constitute a medical treatment.

By the sixteenth century herbs had a commercial life all their own. The nonmonastic apothecary, or "physick", garden, whose main purpose was to grow plants from which essential oils could be distilled, came into being. There was always a pharmacy located nearby, where apothecaries mixed up tinctures and ointments. These establishments were patronized by physicians and, like the monasteries before them, also had infirmaries set up nearby to care for the sick.

With the development of printing, botanical knowledge became easily disseminated through herbals, and herbalism took off on an even greater scale. The herbals contained botanical descriptions and drawings of plants and indicated where they could be found and how they could be used medically. They also referred to the "vertues," or cosmetic and culinary uses. Since printing presses developed first in these countries and interest in herbal cures was strong there, most sixteenth-century herbals are of English or German origin.

Otto Brunfels's *Herbarum Vivae Eicones* (1530) and Leonhard Fuchs's *De Historia Stirpium* (1542) are important documents because the illustrations were drawn from actual specimens. Previous herbals—such as the *Herbarium,* by the Italian Apuleius

Platonicus, printed in 1481 and partially plagiarized from a ninth-century Italian manuscript—contained illustrations of fabulous plants not occurring in nature.

The Englishman John Gerard followed in the new, improved herbal tradition with his *Herball or Generall Historie of Plantes* (1597), often referred to simply as *The Herball*. Although he stretched the truth regarding many details of plants, sampling equally from fact and folklore, he is perhaps most criticized for having borrowed quite a bit of material from another herbal, by Rembert Dodoens, and claiming it as his own. Then the English herbalist John Parkinson published his massive *Theatrum Botanicum* in 1640, sampling too from folklore and other herbals and drawing on his own robust imagination. He even regressed into the territory of fantastical, nonexistent plants that had marred earlier herbals—such as giant plants that grow into animal shapes.

The most notorious of the herbal authors was the Englishman Nicholas Culpeper. His *The Complete Herball* of 1651 diverged from the standard format of medicinal, household, and culinary information about plants. A part-time practicing astrologer, the eccentric Culpeper spiced his prose with celestial ramblings—and he did so with such conviction and enthusiasm that even today it is difficult not to believe his claims. Of the herb southernwood, for instance, he writes: "It is a gallant Mercurial plant.... The ashes mingled with old salad oil, restoreth the hair—and cureth baldness."

During the sixteenth and seventeenth centuries astrology, medicine, and herbs became strongly linked. Five planets had been named and discovered at that time—

On Midsummer Day in Sweden, herbal flower crowns can be found strewn on the rocks of Åles Stennar, a Viking sacred site, opposite. Unmarried women wear the crowns the night before to magically see their future husbands. A Swedish garden, right, entices visitors with scents of June roses.

Neptune, Uranus, and Pluto were still distant, anonymous points of light—and the Earth was not included among them. (The Ptolemaic system, which held that the Earth was at the center of the universe, still had many believers.) Each planet, as well as the sun and the moon, was assigned a part of the body—for example, the sun ruled the heart; the moon governed the breast and stomach. Planets were associated with zodiac

signs, which also corresponded to body parts. Further, herbs were matched with zodiac signs or planets, and a whole system of astrological correspondences resulted. No one knows for certain how herbs became associated with different planets or signs, but it is probably related to the Doctrine of Signatures approach—a yellow flower would naturally be ruled by the sun.

Culpeper subscribed to the plant-and-planet theory wholeheartedly. For example, when discussing the "Government and Vertues" of the daisy, he wrote: "The herb is under the sign of Cancer, and under the dominion of Venus, and therefore good for wounds in the breast, and very fitting to be kept both in oils, ointments, plasters, and syrup." A student of medieval alchemy, he also included a Table of Temperaments, indicating the nature of each plant—hot, dry, cold, or moist—an ancient way of indicating a Type A or B personality.

While it is easy to derive amusement from Culpeper's work from our twentieth-century perspective, we should credit him for his thoroughness in cataloging plants thought to have herbal usages, and for some sound advice. Of the highly toxic herb henbane, for example, he wrote: "Take notice, that this herb must never be taken inwardly." Certainly his herbal must have introduced many genuinely useful herbs to the layman, but his death by consumption at age thirty-eight is reminder enough of the limits of his healing ability.

Revolutionary when it came to established ways, Culpeper also translated the entire *London Pharmacopoeia*—the Bible of physicians—from Latin (the medical language) to English and published an unauthorized version available to the apothecary and commoner. This broke the physicians' monopoly on herbal cures and seemed as much of a giant step for home remedies as the cheap availability of aspirin is for us today.

LINNAEAN TIMES

In the seventeenth century the study of plants took a more scientific turn. Expeditions from Britain in search of new plants were common, beginning with John Tradescant and his son early in the century and followed by a host of other explorers. The Chelsea Physic Garden was established in 1673 by the Society of Apothecaries in London. The apothecaries were anxious to explore all of the possibilities for the exotic new plants as healing agents. The garden's site, near the Thames, was selected because many of the exotic plants had been brought in by plant hunters from the Mediterranean and required a southern exposure. The boats on which they were shipped could be moored adjacent to the garden. (A later embankment, built in 1874, now blocks the garden from the river.)

Carl von Linné, known to English-speakers as Linnaeus, visited the garden in 1736. The Swedish naturalist was working out the details of a complex system by which to name plants. He had published his *Systema Naturae* the previous year, and in 1737 would come out with *Genera Plantarum*. He offered for the first time a consistent rule system for describing and naming plants. His *Species Plantarum* was published in 1753. In it plants were assigned the binomial nomenclature (genus and species) we use today. Linnaeus wasn't all business, though. He named plants based on their classification within a genus, but he often called horrendous-looking plants after his enemies or beautiful ones after friends and patrons! Before Linnaeus, plants listed in the herbals had long descriptive, overlapping Latin names and a multitude of common names, which varied from language to language and region to region. These names were descriptive of their appearance or use: heartsease for the heart-therapeutic *Viola;* eyebright for the purported eye-healing *Euphrasia*. Those older names survive as some of the common names we still use, although, as any novice gardener knows, one common name might apply to two or more different plants—such as "marigold" for both *Calendula* and *Tagetes*.

Although Linnaeus certainly did not discover sexuality in plants, he was the first to understand its significance in a plant's workings. Linnaeus seemed to understand plants intimately, and in his writings—"The Nuptials of Plants," "The Sleep of Plants"—he made their habits seem human. Later, as the professor of medicine at Uppsala University in Sweden, Linnaeus preached a healthy diet of vegetables and fresh curative herbs (despite his penchant for pipe smoking and potfuls of coffee). He became something of a botanical Pied Piper for

Uppsala residents, leading them off into the fields to hear his lectures on wild herbs and other plants of the Swedish countryside; he invigorated botany to the extent that it became popular entertainment. People were, no doubt, enthralled by his frank discussions of plant sexuality and the way he related their reproductive parts to those of humans.

HERBS IN THE NEW WORLD

When the first colonists arrived in North America, they referred to the Native Americans as savages. This is particularly absurd in light of the complexity and accuracy of Native American medicine—and the relative voodooism of the European remedies of the day. The Native Americans had developed sophisticated folk healing practices using the plants of North America. They employed the mayapple to check cancerous growth, a practice later adopted by traditional Western medicine; they powdered the roots of goldenseal as an antidote to allergic infections, still practiced by the herbally minded; used witch hazel for insect bites; and ate the vitamin C–rich raw bulbs of wild garlic as a scurvy preventive. The Native Americans also had developed ingenious culinary techniques, such as seasoning cakes with wild ginger roots and using bee balm and mint leaves to season and preserve dried meat, to name a few.

After the disastrous winter of 1609–1610 in which only sixty of the original five hundred Jamestown colonists survived, they turned to the natives for advice on how to put the plants of North America to best use. They wisely adopted many of the Native American techniques but "Englished" them, integrating them with herbal cures found in the herbals of Culpeper and Parkinson, which they had brought with them.

Elsewhere in the Colonies, settlers cultivated vegetables, fruit, and a multitude of herbs. Licorice, tarragon, lemon balm, mint, borage, chamomile, sorrel, and

lavender are a small sampling of the long list they grew. To these they added flowers, including hollyhocks and lilies, and edged their beds with boxwood.

For years there was no commercial herbalism in America. But the arrival of the Shakers, or members of the United Society of Believers in Christ's Second Appearing, changed all that. They had broken from the Quaker sect in England and established themselves in New York State in 1776. Like the monks of the Middle Ages, the Shakers' goal was to be self-sufficient. They built their store of information on earlier Colonial findings, the wisdom of the Native Americans, and their own observations.

At first the Shakers gathered wild herbs from the woods, but in time they brought the plants into cultivation in home garden plots. The plots grew into farms, and by 1830 they were doing a large-scale advertising campaign for their herbs via fliers and catalogs asking the question "Why send to Europe's bloody shores / For plants which grow by our own doors?" By the end of the nineteenth century the Shakers had secured an advertising agent in New York, and Shaker almanacs were being published. These were surprisingly slick publications offering such products as Pain King (containing, among other herbs, peppermint and opium), Mother Seigel's Curative Syrup for Dyspepsia, and Brown's Extract of English Valerian, which was sold as "the best remedy yet discovered for the cure of Nervousness, Lowness of Spirits, Debility, Hypochondria, Neuralgia, Hysteria, Tic Douloureux, Sick Headache, and every other disease arising from mental affection and nervous exhaustion." There was probably a great deal of truth in that advertisement, considering that valerian produces a narcotic, calming drug.

But by the first decades of the twentieth century many of the Shaker communities in New York and New England had dissolved, although a few are still active today. The beautiful packaging—usually graceful glass bottles or pretty tins with

meticulous labels, sometimes containing an explanation of the contents in several languages—they used and their thoroughness in all aspects of the preparation were refinements to the herbal trade.

We are now the heirs to five thousand years of herbal writing and a tradition of usage extending into the distant past, when early peoples lived on a harsher, more forbidding Earth and needed to unlock the secrets of its plants in order to survive. The medical and botanical sciences have cataloged and categorized a great many of the Earth's plants, laying bare their herbal secrets. Still, when we contemplate the remarkable tradition behind these herbs and all they contribute to our lives, we can derive a newfound respect for them—these humble plants that grow so easily and obligingly in our gardens.

The Trie Garden at Manhattan's Cloisters, above, takes inspiration from the gardens depicted in the medieval The Hunt of the Unicorn *tapestry. Yellow flag iris, once used as a common European household dye, is featured here.*

CHAPTER ONE

HERB
GARDENING

Despite their rich history, most people are unsure of how, exactly, to define herbs. *Herbs* is a word that can be used in different ways. (And, for that matter, pronounced in different ways, too: in England *herb* starts with a pronounced "h", whereas on American shores the "h" sound is absent.) In the botanical sense an herb is a plant without a permanent woody stem that dies back to the ground after flowering. This definition, however, is of little concern to the historic herb gardener. Herbs in the historical sense—and in the context of this book—are plants used as food, flavoring, medicine, fragrance, or in some utilitarian way in the household. In many cases the herb is no longer employed in the way it once was and may now serve a purely decorative function. Still, we value old-fashioned herbs for their historic significance and for their prominent place in the lives of people of bygone times.

The French term *fines herbes* signifies a mix of herbs—usually four—combined to season a dish; the combinations vary depending on what they are flavoring but usually involve savories, basil, chives, parsley, sage, thyme, and sweet marjoram. Herbs are distinguished from vegetables in that they are not the primary ingredient of a dish but are used in a supplementary way to season it. There are delightful exceptions, such as a salad made purely of edible herbs and blossoms.

The types of herbs you choose to grow depend on what you hope to derive from your garden. If you are a cook, then a culinary plot is a must, brimming with the charming, traditional herbs employed so artfully in the dishes of the past. Armed with training in the use of herbs and a heavy dose of caution, you might attempt a

Rosemary and basil conform to circle and ball-like shapes, right, at Well-Sweep Herb Farm in New Jersey. Boxwood, once used to treat rheumatism, defines the edges of the Morris Jumel Mansion in New York, opposite left. A bay tree topiary, opposite right, grows in a container and can be easily removed for grass mowing.

medicinal herb garden. Contemporary medicinal gardens most often grow plants that can be used for soothing and beautifying lotions and rinses or for tonic teas. In such a garden you might grow curious plants that once were used to cure maladies of the body and spirit but that are enjoyed today for their appearance rather than for usefulness. For people who are skilled at handicrafts a household garden is a treat. It yields raw materials for an endless list of crafts—dyeing, potpourri, tussie-mussies, sachets, and the like. Since many herbs can be used in several ways, it's best to become familiar with all of them and perhaps find several uses for each plant. Never forget that an herb garden is not strictly utilitarian in an active sense. Above all you can enjoy it for itself—just contemplating it and savoring its fragrance.

PLANTING THE GARDEN

Once you have decided on your objectives, it's time to decide which plants to grow. For herbs that can be used as flavorings for food, you have an enormous selection. But let the following be your primer.

Anise makes a wonderful flavoring for cakes; balm, chervil, and rosemary add interest to chicken dishes; coriander and mint infuse sauces with their own distinctive flavors; horseradish and lovage pair admirably with beef; hyssop, lovage, bay, and fennel enrich soups; lemon thyme, lemon verbena, and sweet cicely accompany fruits; marjoram and costmary enliven peas; and summer savory, tarragon, and thyme complement fish.

The tender young leaves of many herbs add interesting flavor to salads and have a long culinary tradition. They should be used sparingly, along with such greens as butter lettuce, watercress, and chicory. Choices include the basils, borage, dandelion, bee balm, young shoots of Good King Henry, alpine strawberry, parsley, and French sorrel. The leaves and flowers of chives, chicory, hollyhock, marigold, dill, salad rocket (arugula), and nasturtium can be used in the same way. In the case of heartsease, use the flowers alone.

For soothing herbal teas, grow the following: chamomile, catnip, apple mint, hyssop (reputedly great for the common cold), sage, and peppermint. If you envision your herb garden yielding material for luxurious baths, cultivate angelica, lavender, bee balm, mugwort, feverfew, and roses. You can tie up the dried herbs in muslin or cotton bags and let bath water run over them. Fragrant herbs for the time-honored practices of potpourri, sachets, or pillows include sage, hops, scented geraniums, roses, southernwood, pinks, sweet flag, and hyssop.

In the past, plant-based dyes were found to bring vivid hues or delicate pastel shades to fabric. Plants for the dye garden include dyer's broom, woad, indigo, madder, safflower, and dyer's weld. Any connoisseur of Persian rugs knows that the richest, most lively hues are the result of natural dyes.

Herbs have another practical application—as organic insect repellents! The plants to harvest for this worthy purpose are rosemary, southernwood, wormwood, tansy, garlic, chives, lavenders, and sages.

To anyone who loves herbs, all herbs are beautiful, but if beauty is more important to you than usefulness, try some of these: borage, which will yield gorgeous blue flowers; lavender, for its misty violet blooms; foxglove, an old medicinal herb with beautiful spires of purple, pink, or white blossoms; chives and other *Allium* species plants, whose showy round flower heads bring diversity to the herb garden; roses, for their perfect petals; pot marigolds and nasturtiums for a jolt of bright orange, red, or yellow; clary sage, for its beautiful woolly leaves and appealing flowers; and poppies, chamomile, bee balm, violets, and sweet rocket for their striking blooms.

An herb garden stressing interesting foliage could include the variegated-leaf varieties of balm, apple mint, and rue; the golden-leaf varieties of marjoram, thyme, and sage; and the silvery foliage of artemisia, catmint, curry plant, and French thyme. Add additional surges of blues, purples, and grays with borage, hyssop, lavender, and rue. Plant selection in herb gardens also rests heavily on the design of the garden; turn to page 36 to read more about this subject before settling on a planting scheme.

Herb knots—such as this one featuring lavender, catmint, germander, boxwood, and creeping thyme—are a classic design still viable today, below. Their orderly rows make harvesting simple. In a more informal garden, opposite, herbs such as valerian and pasque flower spill luxuriantly over pathways.

Another consideration in planting your herb garden is strictly a matter of patience. If you wish quick results, you should probably consider the annual herbs. Annuals are plants that live for one season and die after setting seed. These are grown each year from seeds sown directly in the garden or from tender seedlings you buy at a nursery. Popular annuals include anise, coriander, dill, cumin, pot marigold, summer savory, and sweet basil. If you plant seeds in May, you can begin harvesting by August.

Other herbs are biennials—they live for two years, usually flower in the second season, and die after setting seed. Caraway, clary sage, and parsley are members of this category. The first two cannot be harvested the first year, but parsley can because it is cultivated for its leaves rather than its seed.

Other herbs are perennials—they live for several years, dying back in winter but reawakening in spring. Lemon balm, catnip, costmary, hyssop, lavender, lovage, marjoram, oregano, pennyroyal, peppermint, rosemary, sage, tansy, tarragon, and thyme fit this category.

For quick results, raise some annuals from seed and transplant biennial and

For centuries, herbs have been grown in pots and urns, left and above. Hundreds of seeds await planting and judicious watering in a well-drained soil, opposite above and below.

perennial plants bought from a nursery. Since transplants are more expensive than growing from seed, you might also set aside a patch for seeding your own perennials.

CHOOSING A SITE

People love herbs because they grow so easily; even the most difficult garden can be home to at least one herb. But before you plant, and once you have a list of herbs to plant in mind, you should walk around your property to find the best location for your herb garden. Generally speaking, herbs are not difficult to grow, but they do tend to favor a level, sunny spot where they can receive about five hours of sunlight a day balanced by some shade during the daylight hours. They should be somewhat protected from wind and not be located on a low point in the property, which can be a potential frost pocket. A sun-filled courtyard enclosed by walls, in the manner of the medieval monasteries, would be an ideal location because it provides wind protection for the herbs year-round and captures warmth during the cooler months when the plants are above ground. Take note of potential shadow casters, such as trees and shrubbery.

If you can't accommodate a sunny herb patch on your property, consider gearing the garden to the more shade-tolerant herbs: monkshood, angelica, bistort, burdock, chervil, the tenacious dandelion, feverfew, foxglove, golden marjoram, sorrel, sweet cicely, valerian, and wintergreen. (For all those gardeners who have plenty of dandelions without even trying, consider that Culpeper wrote: "Great are the virtues of this common herb, and that is the reason the French and Dutch so often eat them in the spring." The dandelion has also been an herb of the aristocracy. James II [reigned 1685–1688] enjoyed dandelion leaves in his salads, and eighteenth-century Prussian nobles were known to use the herb medicinally to treat dropsy and iron deficiencies.)

SOIL

The soil for herbs should be of average quality, neither devoid of nor too rich in organic material. For the widest possible choice of plants to grow, an herb garden should be well drained, so make sure it is located where waterlogging is not a problem. If it looks as though a very damp herb garden is unavoidable, grow herbs that tolerate dampness: monkshood, angelica, balm, bee balm, bistort, chives, comfrey, mints, sweet cicely, sweet flag, valerian, and violets. Mediterranean herbs—such as sage, thyme, lavender, and rosemary—prefer a light soil and do not require additional nutrients.

You can analyze the soil with a soil test kit or, if you are a United States resident, by contacting your local cooperative extension service to make arrangements to have the soil tested for you. If the soil is so nutrient-poor that you feel you have to add fertilizer, do so, but with a light touch. The goal, especially with a culinary herb garden, is not

to produce luxuriant, bushy plants but compact ones whose energy has been channeled into producing leaves and flowers redolent with scent and flavor. If you must fertilize, opt for garden compost, manure, wood ashes, or medium-grade bonemeal. A very dry, sandy soil might benefit from an application of perlite to help it retain water.

GROWING FROM SEED

Before planting, turn the soil over in late summer or early autumn. This will make it more friable in spring when it's time to sow seeds. If you choose to sow seeds directly into the garden, do so in early spring after the danger of frost has passed. Broadcast them over the area and rake them into the soil. Make sure the seedlings get watered if you hit a spell of dry weather. Watering is more important for seedlings than it is for fully grown plants. When seedlings begin to emerge, thin out congested areas so that they don't become sickly.

Some gardeners like to start their seedlings indoors in late winter to give them that extra advantage during their first few weeks of life. This practice is particularly useful in cold climates, where the last frost date is late in the spring. Some people like to start seedlings in a greenhouse, but any area where the ratio of light to heat is balanced will work. You should sow them in trays filled with seed compost, cover the trays with newspaper to keep them in the dark, and, as with seeds sown outdoors, thin out seedlings spaced too closely together when they begin to emerge. Remove the newspaper when the seedlings begin to push through the compost. Move them into the garden in May or after the danger of frost has passed.

A Manhattan garden, opposite, designed by Cahill & Gardner, testifies to the resilience of herbs in urban settings. Most Allium species plants are grown easily from bulbs planted in autumn or seeds sown in spring, above right. The thorough gardener takes the time to germinate seeds indoors in the greenhouse, below right.

Transplants taken from a nursery or your own windowsill and put out in spring yield quick results. This is a fairly simple process: with delicacy, remove the plant from its container, place it in the ground, fanning out the roots and removing damaged ones, replace soil and pat it down with a spade or your foot, water it, and add manure as necessary. Keep an eye on the plants until a comfortable margin of time goes by, about a month. Plants can also be raised from stem cuttings (which are lateral shoots) taken in summer. Rosemary, geraniums, hyssop, and sages are good candidates for this procedure because their cuttings tend to be durable. To take a cutting, use a sharp knife to remove the shoot, strip the bottom portion of leaves, and dip the cutting in a rooting liquid—a hormone-infused mixture that encourages the plant to root. Bury the cutting up to one-and-a-half inches in a seed tray. You will know the cutting has rooted successfully when it shows signs of new growth.

GARDEN MAINTENANCE

Once your herb garden is planted, it doesn't require the intense upkeep that some styles of gardening demand: In keeping with their helpful personalities, herbs are self-reliant plants with few pressing needs. Perhaps the most consistent and laborious chore of all is weeding, and because at least part of your herb garden is likely to contain culinary herbs, the use of herbicides to treat pests and diseases is not advisable. This leaves the option of weeding the old-fashioned way: by hand. As you weed, take the opportunity to rummage through the underbrush of your herb garden, removing decayed plant matter. Many plants will bloom a second time if you remove old flower heads. Of course, if you want to collect seed from the flowers, as with sunflowers, leave them on the plant. There are some herbs that shouldn't be allowed to flower at all if you want maximum benefits from their other parts. This especially applies to sage and Russian tarragon.

Each season in the herb garden requires different activities. In late winter or early spring, survey the garden for plants that have suffered upward heaving as a result of cold soil and tamp them back into the ground. It is a prime time to apply fertilizer lightly, using garden compost, manure, wood ashes, or medium-grade bonemeal. Early spring is also the time to take precautionary measures against pests and diseases in the rest of your garden, although you will find that few pests and diseases affect herbs. Perhaps it is this charmed quality that inspired ancient peoples to believe in their powers. Some herbs are natural insect repellents and will help keep your garden healthy. But there are two pests that daunt even the most skilled gardener: slugs and snails. These particularly voracious creatures like to feed on just about any part of an herb plant, particularly in dark or wet areas of the garden. Slug pellets should do the trick to repel them. So will shallow dishes containing beer, a drink slugs can't resist and in which they invariably—and happily—drown. If you keep your garden in good order—picking up old leaves and weeding regularly—all should be well. In

Some gardeners prefer watering by hand to automated systems in order to give individual attention to each plant, left. Herbs form the cornerstone of the Culpeper Garden at Leeds Castle, opposite. Distant relatives of the famous herbalist once lived here.

spring you will find the appearance of the garden much improved if you prune shrubby herbs such as rosemary, lavender, sage, and santolina.

Your pruning chores will continue right into summer if you have a more formal herb garden. Knots and geometric shapes require regular attention to be kept in line. Though you may be tempted to water frequently throughout the summer, fight the impulse unless the weather has been especially dry. Most herbs are native to dry climates and simply don't need a lot of water; if they get too much, they will be subject to dreaded damping-off disease, which develops from excess moisture. A suitably old-fashioned way to collect water for the herb garden is to add a rain barrel nearby; with a rain barrel and a watering can your herbs will get all the water they need.

Herb gardens also benefit from a mulching in summer and winter. A mulch is an organic material—such as peat moss, decomposed leaves, straw, pine bark mulch or shredded hardwood bark (both supplemented by lime and nitrogen), buckwheat hulls, and cocoa shells—used to cover the soil around the plants. Mulching in summer performs many functions: it keeps the soil in the beds moist, prevents weed seed from germinating and smothers weeds that have already started to grow, and prevents soil from dispersing. Some people find slugs to be a problem when they mulch; to combat this, create "a beer garden" as described earlier. Mulching in winter protects perennial herb plants by maintaining an even temperature in the beds, which counteracts freezing and thawing.

GARDENING WITH CONTAINERS

Containers look beautiful and make herb gardening versatile. They can be picked up and moved around as you see fit, scenting a corner of a patio one day and creating

landscape accents the next. Good container plants are purple sage, yarrow, and chives.

Any number of reasons spur the gardener to take advantage of the herb's natural penchant for containers. If cooking with fresh herbs is indispensable to you, but running to the herb garden every time you want a snipping is too much trouble, individual pots of herbs on the windowsill or one container large enough to support a colony of several herbs will suit your needs. If you opt for the large barrel, suggested plantings include pot marjoram, basil, thyme, and parsley, perhaps mixed with some nasturtiums for color, or sage, oregano, rosemary, several types of peppermint, and calendulas. Or try a more dramatic arrangement of lavender or fennel in the center surrounded by more low-lying herbs such as parsley and creeping thyme, which can wend its way over the sides of the container in classical ivy fashion. If you live in a northern clime, it is an especially good idea to use the fragrant-leaved geraniums

and rosemary as container plants, since you can bring them indoors in winter.

Don't think that because you are planting in a container the soil does not need to be maintained. You must add a good compost, preferably a type available commercially, which is free of the latent weeds and bacteria lurking in compost created from your own garden. Be more vigilant about watering a container than you would a garden, because containers retain considerably less moisture. The container must have drainage. If you have found a really stunning container to use—a bamboo-patterned glazed Chinese pot or a classical stone urn—but it has no drainage hole, add broken crockery to the bottom; this will allow drainage.

The cottage garden at Eyhorne Manor looks delightful with its container plantings of golden thyme, lavender, and curry plant, opposite. Herbs growing in an old trough instantly evoke a sense of the past in the herb garden at Acorn Bank in England, above.

URBAN HERB GARDENING

If you are an urbanite, don't despair over the lack of space for a full-scale herb garden. If you have access to a roof or balcony, try growing herbs in containers out there. Consider the long tradition of urban herb cultivation, to give your activity a vintage quality. This century is certainly not the first to appreciate the merits of gardening in containers; their use in the past was relegated mostly to cities.

In the ancient Near East, city dwellers tended container gardens on their rooftops. Greeks and Romans later copied the practice, dedicating these rooftop oases to different deities, who were symbolized in the vegetation. The Greeks, in particular, favored growing roses in their "Gardens of Adonis." The Romans used a broad selection of pots and went so far as to plant fruit trees and install fish ponds in these urban spaces. In Italy a millennium later, window boxes became popular for herbal and floral plantings. Pompeians grew their herbs in large terra-cotta pots, which endured burial in volcanic ash for centuries. All had drainage holes! By medieval times in Europe earthenware and painted metal containers were placed directly in the garden. In the New World private Aztec homes had sophisticated courtyard and roof gardens that grew useful plants of all kinds. This made such an impression on the Spanish conquistadores that they sent word home of this unusual way to garden.

The courtyard garden can be a lot of fun. Take advantage of urban architecture by giving your small herb plot a classical, formal air. Knots are excellent choices for this situation.

If you have no choice but to grow herbs indoors, make sure they are situated where they will get a lot of sun. One potential problem is exposure to excess heat from indoor radiators and a lack of light in winter. Try to find a middle ground, a room in which the heat is not intense but the plants still get light. In the winter a southern exposure is a good choice, but you may find that a southeastern, southwestern, or eastern exposure serves better in warmer months. Good choices for the culinary windowsill are anise, basil, chervil, chives, marjoram, mint, tarragon, and thyme. Try adding the rose-scented geranium—a classic window box plant—for color and also for the use of the leaves and flowers in jams and fruit drinks.

Santolina, a household herb once strewn on floors mixed with rushes to scent and sanitize them, creates a pleasant meadow-like effect at London's Chelsea Physic Garden, below. Container herbs are grown at Iden Croft Herbs in England, opposite, so as to be easily transported to gardens and sunny city window boxes.

HERB GARDEN DESIGN

Herbs dress up or down and will look lovely in any context in which you use them. There is such variety in growing form among herbs and such textural complexity in their foliage that creating a composition with them affords you great freedom. Many have compact shapes and grow in low mats. Others have more upright habits, and some can be sheared into hedges. Designing an interplay of these elements is the challenge of the herb garden.

If you don't have enough space for a separate herb garden but already have some plantings on your property, it is possible to integrate herbs with them. You can devote a few rows of the vegetable garden to herbs.

Or add herbs to the border, where they can share quarters with other herbaceous plants. As a rule in borders, taller-growing plants, such as fennel and angelica, should be planted in the background, with the lower-growing herbs, tansy or parsley, for example, featured in the front. But the border does not need to be a straight line against a wall. An island border, set in the middle of the property, can undulate in drifts, with the higher-growing plants curving through the center.

Herb gardens in the informal cottage style are serene, fragrant places, replete with stands of lavender, masses of purple-flowering chives, and climbing roses. Keep in mind, though, that this type of herb garden can take on an aimless, rangy look if you don't give it some structure, however subtle. You need to be able to move through the garden without disturbing plants in order to harvest them. Gravel, mulch, earth, or grass pathways are all at home in the informal herb garden. If you use stone pathways, allow herbs to grow between spaces in them and spill out onto them. Simple fences can define areas of the garden. You can also build a low wall out of native stone and allow creeping thyme and savories to clothe it with fragrance.

Other designs to consider are geometric—but not necessarily stiff—forms. The spiral is an interesting one. You simply dig a long, continuous trench that winds around itself. Clear the ground and plant herbs on the raised, undug part, which should be about two feet across. It is easy to walk through the trenches to plant and harvest, and children can be easily induced to work in the spiral garden because walking through it is like playing a game.

Additional shapes to consider are the half-moon and the triangle. These garden styles are easy to create because they don't require putting in paths, but they have to be kept small so that you can reach in easily to harvest the herbs. If you want a more open design, consider a cartwheel of radiating herb beds bordered by paved paths. At the center, add a focal point such as a bee skep

or fountain, or a living focal point such as boxwood trimmed into a topiary shape.

VINTAGE DESIGNS

Part of the pleasure in growing herbs is derived from their long tradition in the garden. It can be gratifying to plant herbs in the same types of designs as they were in the past. In medieval times, as the traditions of chivalry, knighthood, and courtly love developed, the garden became a paradisal bower designed for pleasurable, leisurely pursuits. Noblemen and their ladies kept company in the "flowery meads" of these gardens—reclining on a carpet of scented ground covers. The traditional choice was chamomile, a compact, low-growing herb that releases a lovely scent when you tread on it. Later, in the seventeenth century, people still walked or dozed on beds of chamomile, but chamomile also grew on turf seats!

If you are bored with the traditional suburban swath of green, why not plant a scented lawn of chamomile, pennyroyal, or creeping thyme? Flowering Roman chamomile is a cushiony herb with delicate creamy white blossoms and is best planted in areas where there is not constant foot traffic, such as the edges of paths or in wild areas of your property. Pennyroyal, whose fragrance is akin to peppermint, also does best in somewhat isolated areas. The creeping thymes are wonderful for stabilizing slopes and for spreading out over rocky areas. Nonflowering Roman chamomile is best in large areas that are well trodden.

Another medieval innovation was the embroidery, or knot, garden. Growing out of the monastic tradition of geometric, orderly beds, these gardens were composed of manicured herb hedges that intersected to form a pattern akin to interwoven ropes. Herbal foliages of varying shades of gray and green were used. Inside the beds grew other herbs and flowers.

The knot tradition took even more fanciful twists in Tudor times. It was usually square, the exterior defined by boxwood or santolina, the interior containing complex

knots or ribbons of the same border material. Interwoven lines created a closed knot, while nonconnecting lines created an open knot. Rather than herbs, colored earth or sand was used between the knots to heighten the fantasy ornamental effect. The knot became a curiosity meant to be viewed from a higher elevation, such as the upper floors of a grand house or an artificial mount on the property.

The knot has much to recommend it. It does not have to be a very large garden to be visually effective. You can design a simple square defined by lavender, rue, rosemary, hyssop, cotton lavender, germander, or boxwood, place an interesting herb like catmint in the center as a focal point, and create lines of lavender radiating from the focal point to the corners of the square. Fill in the spaces in between with ground-hugging herbs like shepherd's thyme, pennyroyal, and chamomile.

HARVESTING HERBS FOR CULINARY USES

Even small herb gardens tend to be so prolific that it is difficult to keep pace with an entire spring and summer's production. Inevitably you will want to harvest greens and flowers to preserve for winter use. Your primary goal is for your dried herb to resemble its fresh state as closely as possible by retaining the aroma and flavor of the live plant. To ensure these results, you must pluck the herb at the optimum time: when the plants are richest in essential oils. This is generally just before the plant flowers; after flowering, herbs have considerably less volatile oils present. You'll know a plant is about to flower because of the presence of buds.

In herbal folklore, harvesting by the full moon is said to invest the plants with

Knots of sculpted boxwood enclose old-fashioned herbs at the Tradescant Garden in London, opposite. Plants grown in this garden were all known to John Tradescant the Elder and Younger, the famous seventeenth-century plant explorers.

magical flowers, turning single-flower forms into double forms or guaranteeing that the flowers will never fade and the foliage never wilt. But it's actually best to harvest in the morning after the dew has evaporated from the plants but before the sun has climbed high in the sky.

To harvest leaves, go out into the garden with a basket in hand and, using a sharp knife, begin plucking one type of herb at a time, until you have gathered all you will be able to convert efficiently and quickly to a preserved state.

To harvest flowers, pick them just as they are opening. Place them in a single layer in a basket. To harvest seeds, wait until they turn brown on the plant. Seeds can fall off very easily, so handle the seed-bearing plants very carefully.

DRYING AND PRESERVING

Dry your herbs in a dark, well-ventilated place with a temperature ranging from 70 degrees Fahrenheit (21 degrees Celsius) to 90 degrees Fahrenheit (32 degrees Celsius). You may opt for an airing cupboard or just a small, dark room. The herbs will vary in drying times—usually within one week—so this is something you must keep track of. To dry them, either hang the herbs upside down loosely bound in bunches or spread them thinly on wire mesh. Stir the herbs on the mesh every day to promote even drying. The plants are dry when they feel dry to the touch but do not crumble to pieces. As soon as the herbs are dry, remove the leaves from the stems. Immediately place the dried herbs in clean, airtight storage jars—tin canisters and blue mason jars work well. Label and date the contents so that you'll use your herbs in order of freshness. Store them out of light to preserve freshness.

Flowers and leaves for potpourri should be dried on screens as described above. If you wish to dry flowers or foliage whole, dry them upside down or suspend them upright through chicken wire hung from the ceiling.

To obtain seeds from plants, hang them upside down over paper so that the seeds can fall onto it; alternatively, upon harvesting seed plants, invert them immediately into brown paper bags so that the seeds will drop as they dry.

You can also freeze a number of culinary herbs—in particular basil, chervil, chives, dill, fennel, lovage, marjoram, mint, parsley, salad burnet, sorrel, and French tarragon. These freeze well because they have soft leaves. You can use these frozen herbs in recipes that call for fresh leaves. To collect herbs for freezing, go out into the garden earlier than you would to collect herbs for drying. You want the dew to still be on the plants. Collect the plants, bring them indoors, wash them, and shake them dry. Then place them in freezer storage bags or containers. Or you may want to blanch the herbs before freezing them by immersing them into boiling water for a minute or two and then plunging them into cool water immediately afterward. Store them in small quantities so that you don't have to remove and handle a big bag of herbs every time you want fresh ones.

Golden-leaved marjoram is flanked by French tarragon and spearmint at Wisley Garden, below. The rich red berries of staghorn sumac, once used by North American Indians to soothe sore throats, dry in a barn loft, opposite. This plant can also be hung upside down to dry, as with most herbs.

CHAPTER TWO

CULINARY
HERBS
WITH
RECIPES

The applications of herbs to cooking extend well beyond the perfunctory parsley garnish or a hasty sprinkling of a dried herb in a sauce. Strangely, creating intricate blendings of herbs in food—as with French fines herbes *mixtures and the intimidating-sounding* bouquet garni—*has come to be associated with gourmet cooking and tends to be off-putting to most cooks. This is somewhat ironic considering how very basic and ancient most herbal recipes are, that the herb blendings are such a personal matter and it is difficult to make mistakes.*

Still, herbs have a mystique to them that keeps some people at arm's length when it comes to the kitchen. The fact that many culinary herbs are not available fresh in stores doesn't help the matter and makes them seem even more alien.

Within this chapter, which concerns culinary herbs and their historic usages, is a smattering of recipes created by contemporary cooks, many of them drawing on age-old traditions. The recipes call for dried and fresh herbs, depending on chefs' preferences. Keep in mind that dried herbs are used in a lesser proportion than fresh in recipes. You can substitute one-third to one-half of the amount of dried herbs in recipes that call for fresh herbs and two to three times the amount of fresh herbs for dried. Dried herbs lose flavor as they age, so don't use any that have been sitting on your spice rack for an extended period.

Use the recipes in this chapter as a starting point from which to build your own. To expand your culinary herbal repertoire, consult old cookery sources and reinterpret recipes to suit the contemporary kitchen. Above all, proceed with an understanding and appreciation of the long tradition of culinary herbs.

Billowy, magical-looking rhubarb can serve two purposes, depending on which species is used. Medicinal rhubarb is sometimes prescribed for digestive problems; garden rhubarb is best known as a pie ingredient. Here it grows in Britain's Wisley Garden, right, along with dandelion, an ancient culinary herb. Lamb's quarters, opposite, are a vintage herb cooked just like spinach.

Allium fistulosum
WELSH ONION
Allium schoenoprasum
CHIVES

The ancient, pungent alliums date so far back into antiquity that their first verifiable usages are elusive. They include the well-known onion, garlic, and leek as well as numerous other bulb plants, some edible and others purely ornamental. Two of the most fascinating vintage species, chives and the Welsh onion, are both indigenous to the Orient and have weathered the centuries with remarkably few changes in their herbal applications.

When the Venetian traveler Marco Polo first encountered chives on an extended journey to China in the late thirteenth century, they had already been a culinary staple of life there for at least three thousand years. By the sixteenth century chives had become an established plant in Europe, but even by Culpeper's time they were not so well known in England that the inquiring herbalist had heard of them. He wrote: "I confess I had not added these had it not been for a country gentleman, who, by a letter certified to me that amongst other herbs I had left these out." Although Culpeper did not rave about chives (he felt that they sent "very hurtful vapours" to the brain), they did manage to gain a foothold in Western cooking as an accompaniment to egg, fish, and salad dishes as well as in

The Oxford Botanic Garden, opposite, has attracted many illustrious visitors, including Lewis Carroll (with schoolgirl Alice Liddell in tow), Linnaeus, the diarist Samuel Pepys, and herbalist John Evelyn. Globular Welsh onion, feathery fennel, white-flowered arugula, and yellow elecampane are shown. Chives, a more familiar Allium species, flourish beneath an armillary sphere, right.

stews. Chives even earned the reputation, as did first cousin garlic, of protecting against the evil eye if hung in a room.

The flavor of chives is less pronounced than that of the onion but sweeter. To preserve the beauty of a cluster of chive plants growing in the garden, harvest the spiky leaves from the least visible areas of the plants. The foliage will renew itself. When the plant blooms in mid- to late

summer, you can either harvest the pastel globular flowers or let them remain. The flowers use up vital energy of the plant that could otherwise go into leaf production, but they are so appealing that you may want to leave them for beauty in the garden or even to harvest for dried flower arrangements. (Be prepared for the oniony smell to linger, but it does have the advantage of driving away evil beings.) Enterprising cooks use the flowers as a garnish.

While chives are universally beloved for the delicate beauty they bring to the garden, the Welsh onion seems to inspire scorn. Many people find the coarse, fuzzy white flowers off-putting and shriek, "Off with their heads!" as soon as the blooms appear, giving the entirely valid excuse that the plant needs to channel energy into leaf production, not making flowers. But the flowering plant actually has a stark, ugly-duckling appeal that may strike you immediately or may just grow on you. This allium actually has nothing to do with Wales, as the word *Welsh* is applied in the Old English sense of "foreign." It's less confusing to think of it as the Chinese spring onion; it has been an important herb in Japan and China for millennia.

As might be expected from its compelling appearance, the Chinese spring onion has a much stronger flavor than chives (with hints of onion and garlic) and should be used in the same manner chives are used in cooking, but more sparingly; it is particularly effective as a soup herb. The bulbs can also be used as early green onions. But the Chinese spring onion's history has more to do with its medicinal than its culinary usages. In Chinese herbalism it is known as *cong bai* and is classified as a diaphoretic, a plant with a pungent and warm nature that eases external ailments brought on by exposure to the elements. The fresh plant's stalks and rootlets are made into a paste mixed with honey and used as a salve. It is also made into a decoction with ginger root and sugar that is purported to soothe chills.

The allure of the alliums will surely inspire you to plant them in your herb garden or perhaps even in an Oriental vegetable patch, along with bok choy, mizuna, and Chinese kale. Chives look lovely in the border or as an edging plant; the Chinese spring onion is more imposing and should be planted where it can be enjoyed as a sculptural accent. Both chives and the Chinese spring onion favor full sun. It is especially important to provide chives with

sun, as the slender plants will look gangly and not flower much without it.

These unfussy plants are prominent in the herb garden throughout most of the year. Although chives' leaves die back in the cold seasons, early spring sees new growth as spikelets push optimistically through the soil. The tougher Chinese spring onion has bluish foliage that can even remain on the plant through the winter, fittingly symbolic of the alliums' endurance through the centuries.

Matjes Herring with Chives

Matjes herring—matjes is the Dutch word for virgin—are caught just before the mating season, so they are particularly fat and succulent. Chives and dill both enliven this traditional dish, as prepared at Stallmästaregården, Stockholm, shown at right. Served with some crusty dark bread, beer, and aquavit, it's a memorable meal.

Serves 6.

12–18 small red potatoes, unpeeled
3–4 sprigs dill
12 matjes herring fillets (available canned or in delicatessens)
1 pint sour cream
½ cup chopped chives

Put potatoes, dill, and just enough water to cover in 3-quart saucepan. Bring to a boil, cover, reduce heat slightly and cook 15 to 20 minutes, until potatoes are fork tender; drain. Cut potatoes in half and place in a bowl. Roll up herring fillets and place on a small serving platter. Put sour cream and chives into separate bowls or gravy boats. Serve "family style," allowing each person to help him- or herself to potatoes and herring, adding sour cream and chives as desired.

You can either admire Welsh onion in the garden, left, or use it as a soup herb. If the plants receive plenty of sun, they will develop thick, hollow stalks and grow over a foot high.

Chef Thomas Alf of Leith's Restaurant, London, offers these dishes for a spring or an early summer herbal dinner party, as shown opposite. This menu lends itself particularly well to outdoor dining. The recipes are based on fresh seasonal ingredients and accompanied by your favorite fresh vegetables, this is a repast your guests will never forget. A mixture of dried herbs is used, but you can substitute greater quantities of fresh herbs.

Grilled Spring Lamb with Tomato-Herb Cream Sauce

This dish is a perfect introduction to the joys of cooking with lamb. For anyone who grew up eating lamb as dry and tasteless as shoe leather, try this herb-infused dish and cook it rare or medium, not well done, as the cooks of our childhood tended to do. The meat must be prepared days in advance to achieve the proper seasoning.

The key to success with this dish is the freshest lamb and herbs available and a very hot charcoal fire (which will cook the lamb quickly, keeping the center of the meat tender). To enhance the dish all the more, sprinkle the burning charcoal with dried mixed herbs just before cooking.

To make the mixed dried herbs, mix two tablespoons each of anise, basil, coriander, lavender, mustard seeds, oregano, rosemary, and tarragon in a jar or a bowl. The leftover herb mixture will be a perfect complement to any red meat dish.

Serves 6
1 boned leg of spring lamb (about 3 pounds)

Marinade

2 cups olive oil, or enough to cover the meat
1 clove garlic, halved
1 tablespoon mixed dried herbs

Sauce

2 shallots, chopped
1 cup dry white wine
1 tablespoon white wine vinegar
1 bay leaf
5–6 peppercorns
1 cup heavy cream
1 cup cold unsalted butter, cut into small pieces
2 tomatoes
3 or 4 sprigs each basil, tarragon, chives, and thyme

watercress for garnish

To make marinade: Mix olive oil, garlic, and mixed dried herbs in a medium-sized bowl. Slice leg of lamb into ½-inch-thick steaks. Put them in a large bowl and pour marinade over them. Cover and refrigerate for at least 2 days, preferably 3.

Drain the steaks well; grill over very hot charcoal for about 2 to 3 minutes a side to make the lamb medium-rare, 4 to 5 minutes to make it well done. Remember, the meat continues to cook after you've removed it from the grill, so take the steaks off the fire just before they're cooked the way you want.

To make sauce: In 1-quart saucepan, over medium high heat, bring shallots, wine, vinegar, bay leaf, and peppercorns to a boil. Boil until mixture has reduced to one-third of the original volume. Add cream; whisk in butter until it melts. Strain the mixture through 2 to 3 layers of cheesecloth into a small saucepan and keep warm.

Dip 2 tomatoes in boiling water for 5 seconds. Skin, seed, and dice. Coarsely tear basil, tarragon, chives, and thyme. Add the tomatoes and herbs to the sauce and let stand 5 minutes in a warm place, uncovered.

Spoon the sauce onto a warm plate and arrange the grilled lamb on top. Garnish with watercress.

Grilled Salmon with Chive Butter Sauce

Salmon was a luxury food in the Middle Ages, served at royal banquets from Ireland to France. It was customarily cooked in oil and accompanied by leeks. Nowadays we often serve both a meat and a fish dish as choices for a meal's main course, so here is a variation on this centuries-old favorite, using chives, which are close relatives of the leek; both are members of the Allium genus.

Serves 6

Butter Sauce

2 shallots, finely chopped
1 bay leaf
4 peppercorns
2 cups dry white wine
2 tablespoons white wine vinegar
1 cup heavy cream
½ cup cold unsalted butter, cut into small pieces

6 thin salmon fillets (approximately 5 ounces each)
olive oil
salt and pepper to taste
chopped fresh chives

To make sauce: In 3-quart saucepan, over medium high heat, bring shallots, bay leaf, peppercorns, wine, and vinegar to a boil. Boil until the mixture is reduced to one-quarter of its original volume. Remove from heat. Add heavy cream and cold butter. Reheat over medium low heat, strain, and keep warm.

Brush the salmon with olive oil and season with salt and pepper. Grill the salmon. Depending on how hot your grill is, this will take 30 seconds to over a minute per side. The salmon should be pink in the center.

Ladle the sauce onto a warm plate. Sprinkle liberally with chopped chives. Arrange the salmon on top of the sauce.

Parsley Drop Scones

The traditional British scone is filled with dried fruits, such as raisins, but this unusual version uses parsley as a flavoring. A wonderful savory, the parsley scone makes a nice accompaniment to salmon, smoked fishes, or cheese.

Makes 10 to 12 scones

1¾ cups all-purpose flour
2½ teaspoons double-acting baking powder
1 tablespoon sugar
½ teaspoon salt
6 tablespoons chopped fresh parsley
6 tablespoons butter
2 eggs
⅓ cup milk

Preheat oven to 425 degrees Fahrenheit. Grease large cookie sheet. In medium bowl, mix flour, baking powder, sugar, salt, and parsley. With pastry blender or 2 knives used in scissor fashion, cut in butter until mixture resembles coarse crumbs. In cup, beat eggs; reserve 1 tablespoon. Stir milk into remaining beaten eggs; gently stir egg mixture into flour mixture.

Turn dough onto lightly floured surface; gently roll dough ½-inch thick. With knife, cut dough into 3-inch squares; cut each square into 2 triangles. With pancake turner, place each scone 1 inch apart on cookie sheet; brush with reserved beaten egg. Bake 10 to 15 minutes until golden.

Angelica archangelica
ANGELICA

If one plant could embody perfection, it would have to be all things to all people. And for the medieval-era commoner, angelica was such a plant. It could be eaten for dinner and dessert, deter evil spirits from entering the body, and prevent the plague. Angelica received its name because it seemed a godsend.

Distinctive-looking herbs such as angelica lent themselves readily to the Doctrine of Signatures, the medieval touchstone that held that a plant's appearance gives clues to its usages. Here's how it might have evolved: Angelica has a truly commanding presence. When left to its own devices, it will grow as tall as eight feet high. A member of the Umbelliferae family (sharing bloodlines with the carrot and the herbs dill, caraway, coriander, parsley, and fennel), angelica's wispy umbels of small white or greenish flowers resemble the halos of saints in Christian iconography. Therefore, it was reasoned, the plant, like a lofty guardian, could protect against evil. Angelica has also been associated with the archangel Michael, whose saint day used to be celebrated on the eighth of May—the approximate time of the plant's first bloom.

In varying cultures angelica has been used as a charm against witches, wizards, trolls, ghouls, and pixies. An old British saying goes, "Contagious aire ingendring Pestilence / Infects not those that in their mouth have ta'en / Angelic, that happy counterbane / Sent down from heav'n by some celestial scout / As well the name and nature both avowt." The herb was once hung in Bavarian barns to ward off cattle diseases thought to be spread by evil elves, and European peasants used to wear necklaces

similar purposes. "The wild angelica is not so effective as the garden; although it may be safely used to all the purposes aforesaid," wrote Nicholas Culpeper. These "wild angelicas" vary by continent. In England *A. sylvestris* can be found in moist woodlands, blooming from mid- to late summer; it is not nearly as fragrant as the classic herb-garden angelica.

Angelica's historical culinary uses are just as valid today as they ever were. In medieval times the stalks were candied and the roots were eaten for food and taken medicinally. Scandinavians have been known to eat angelica stem and root raw, perhaps coated with butter. Contemporary cooks blanch the stalks for use as a vegetable, another vintage practice. A stylish variation is to candy the stems; candied angelica stems were the nouvelle cuisine of the eighteenth century, and they do make for quirky dessert garnishes. Or if you wish to sample angelica without all the footwork, try a glass of Chartreuse, which contains distilled oil of angelica root.

To grow angelica from seed, sow only fresh ones, obtained soon after they have ripened; some nurseries can provide fresh seasonal seeds. Angelica is such a striking herb that you should let it define the shape of the herb garden. Grow it in corners to create distinct boundaries or use it as a strong vertical element in a garden of low-growing herbs. The glorious globe-shaped umbels will be as uplifting to your eye as they were to the countryfolk who named the plant for the angels.

made of the plant's foliage to protect themselves when there was evil in the air.

Angelica also has an enticing aroma, further intensifying its otherworldly, mystical associations. In Scandinavia angelica was once used as a muse: poets would don angelica garlands so that they could breathe in its fragrance for inspiration.

John Gerard attempted to explain angelica's healing virtues scientifically in his *Herball or Generall Historie of Plantes:* "It resists poison by defending and comforting the heart, blood, and spirits; it doth the like against the plague and all spirits . . . and all epidemical diseases." In contemporary medicinal usage angelica is employed to treat digestive disorders and as a fortifier against the common cold, taken as tea.

There are other close relatives of the classic garden angelica that have served

A jumble of angelica umbels grows onward and upward in the garden, opposite. The angelic plant happily towers behind a blush of chervil in another garden, above. Because it grows so high (eight feet is standard), this species is best planted behind smaller plants.

Borago officinalis
BORAGE

The dainty hyacinth-blue flowers of borage seem to generate ethereal light from within their petals, even on overcast days. Perhaps this is why this herbal oddity came to be associated with cheerfulness and an ability to lift the spirits. The ancient Roman Pliny the Elder sought giddiness through generous helpings of borage, and sixteen centuries later the herbal author John Gerard recommended using the flowers in salads "to exhilarate." You need not set your sights so high, but do reach for borage when you want to set a happy mood at mealtime. Since the leaves and flowers of borage demand immediate use, they are the perfect herbal combination for summer entertaining.

Revive the garden-party tradition and throw a full-dress event, with borage as a featured ingredient in your menu. Sprinkle borage flowers in a punch bowl or garnish individual glasses of cooling summer drinks with the blossoms for a pretty, lively effect. (The refreshing flowers and leaves were once such a popular addition to beverages in England that the plant took on the curiously unappetizing, industrial-sounding name "cool tankard.") There's no need to worry about guests getting light-headed on borage and running amok through your garden; this herb's mood-lifting abilities are mild.

For the salad course, borage leaves are a lovely treat. The leaves are tastiest when young and can be mixed with vegetables. They are also pleasant in cool summer soups for a light, cucumbery touch. If you're planning on actually cooking for your garden party, you could steam the leaves to serve as a vegetable dish.

Few herbs serve practical and aesthetic needs so fully and gracefully as borage. It is easy to see why the starry blue flowers inspired embroidery design in the Middle Ages. But it is at the same time puzzling why the herb came to be associated with courage. According to the Doctrine of Signatures (the belief that a plant's appearance suggests its usage), one might conclude that borage would help bald men recover their hair, since the leaves are so fuzzy. Or it would seem logical that this fragile-looking, luminescent plant might have some well-placed contacts in the spirit world, and ingesting it might help one see the fairies. But borage, despite its delicacy, was once thought to inspire courage, of all things. Crusaders would take long drinks of borage leaves mixed with wine before sallying forth into battle; women slipped it into their beaux' drinks to encourage marriage proposals; and people drank it whenever they felt fainthearted about some impending challenge. It seems preposterous that such an unassuming plant could have acquired this folkloric baggage, but the world of herbal lore thrives on non sequiturs.

The first settlers in America planted borage widely in their gardens. Perhaps they felt it would embolden them to meet the unknown in the New World. The late-seventeenth-century work *Acetaria, A Discourse of Sallets,* by John Evelyn, was an essential garden reference in the Colonial American and European home. Evelyn wrote that borage sprigs placed in wine "revive the Hypochondriac." Borage was no doubt an excellent placebo for wilderness-weary colonists and a means of motivating tired family members to get out of bed and do some farming.

The distinct wheel shape of borage flowers, opposite, inspired much fancy crewel work in medieval times. Borago is derived from the Latin word burra, meaning hairy or rough, but the plants are more delicate than their name implies. Borage flowers, pineapple mint, and curly spearmint garnish a garden-party punch, right.

Helianthus annuus
SUNFLOWER

The majestic sunflower looms from the misty, ritualistic past of American prehistory—a plant once interwoven in the culture of native tribes spanning the North American Midwest to Peru, where it was placed at the altar of the sun god in ancient Incan temples. Rising as high as ten feet, the sunflower is a living vestige of the past, a floral oddity revered in its native lands and used by ancient peoples of the New World chiefly as a culinary herb but also as a dye and fiber plant.

As part of the sunflower's mystique, it is unknown how this gentle giant inconspicuously made its way to Europe, but it must have tiptoed over—probably in the cargo of Spanish conquistadores traveling back to their homeland with New World plunder. By at least the sixteenth century references to it began to appear in European garden writings. The sunflower caught on immediately in Europe; it seemed a magical plant, the perfect embodiment of the strange New World, which appeared so vast, alien, and exciting. The first recorded description of the sunflower was made in 1569 by a Spaniard, Dr. Monardes (for whom bee balm's genus, *Monarda,* is named under the Linnaean system), in his account of New World plants. Dr. Monardes's writings were later translated into English by John Frampton, who described the sunflower in no uncertain terms as a flower of extraordinary beauty, certainly worth growing in the garden.

Before long, everyone was cultivating sunflowers, enticed by Dr. Monardes's description. John Parkinson was quite taken with it. Ordinarily he was concerned with practical applications for plants. But he was quite willing to overlook this point in the case of the sunflower, or, as he called it, "the golden flower of Peru." He felt that it was gorgeous but had no real usages, although he had heard that "sometimes the heads of the Sunne Flower are dressed and eaten as Hartichokes are . . . but they are too strong for my taste."

Being an extreme-looking plant, the sunflower has naturally fallen in and out of fashion. While Parkinson was infatuated with the sunflower's looks but unaware of its practical uses, others have thought of the plant in the opposite sense. In *Flowers in Britain,* written in 1944, L. H. F. Brimble remarked that "the very large sunflower . . . is not a popular flower because it is ungainly, and never looks attractive except perhaps as a background to a tall, thick herbaceous border." Yet Brimble was well aware of the edible applications of the sunflower seed, having heard of the Russian passion for them, to the extent that the discarded hulls once littered Moscow's streets. Alice Coats also remarks on this usage in her *Flowers and Their Histories* of 1956, saying the seeds are ". . . acceptable to turkeys, parrots, pheasants and Russians."

If you are still ambivalent about the sunflower's visual charms, just remember Vincent van Gogh, whose favorite paint color was yellow. (It's possible that he used

Renaissance-era Europeans immediately embraced the sunflower—the sizable citizen of the New World—and were eager to find uses for it, enchanted by the beauty of its large, disk-shaped heads and vibrant coloration, left and opposite.

foxglove to treat his epilepsy and saw yellow, a side effect of that herb.) Van Gogh never had any qualms about this fabulous flower, and he paid tribute to it with his divine series of sunflower paintings of 1888. The simple drama of the sunflower also inspired Victorians to use it as a motif on everything from teapots to textiles.

Some flowers are so relentlessly happy-looking that it is hard to appreciate them when you are in a sullen mood. But the sunflower has two personalities. At first it is as cheerful as the day, its mischievous heads merrily and optimistically upturned to the sky. Later, as the sunflower winds down and its seeds mature, the heads droop and strike an artistic, studied pose. This duality might induce you to believe it is two different flowers. Both aspects of the sunflower have visual merit and serve your carefree summertime side and your more pensive, autumnal side. Because they grow on the cusp of summer and autumn, sunflowers are perfectly suited to that strange time of year when we are of two minds, one longing for a continual Indian summer, the other battening down for the crisp, demanding days of autumn and all its projects.

You can reap a multiple harvest from your sunflower patch. The protein-rich seeds are easily harvested after you have let the flower head dry in the sun; but act quickly, as birds (and turkeys, parrots, pheasants, and Russians) also love them and will compete with you. Seeds are best gathered in late summer or in autumn, but you must hull them before eating them. Also use the seeds in cookies, muffins, and breads. If you're a real do-it-yourselfer, you can boil the seeds to extract a cooking oil, which will rise to the top of the water. Or forget about cooking entirely and use the unhulled seeds as beads, each one irregular and beautiful, in an old Native American usage.

Being an obliging herb, the sunflower will easily accommodate your vices. Rather than saying you're giving up coffee or smoking, simply announce to family and friends that you've taken up the sunflower.

Civilized cyclopes, sunflowers face the dawn, opposite, at the Blew family farm in New Jersey. The cut flowers make for cheerful arrangements, top. These were nurtured to perfection for Manhattanites to buy at the Union Square Greenmarket. Sunflowers look especially at home in a Native American garden, above. A staple of the Southwest Zuni Indians' diet was sunflower seed pudding.

You must implement this program in late summer or early autumn, when the sunflower is ready for harvest. Then you must follow through. When you crave a cup of coffee, shake loose some sunflower seeds, hull them, isolate the shells, roast them, then grind them, and prepare them as you would coffee. And when the urge to smoke inevitably strikes, carefully dry sunflower leaves in a well-ventilated room and roll them up into cigarettes; the flavor is comparable to mild tobacco. Or simply harvest, dry, and then munch on a few seeds, which will keep your hands busy until the mood passes. If all goes well, this backwoods approach to addictive substances will soon prove wearisome, causing you to associate these habits with *work* and give them up altogether.

Some people deliberate endlessly over where the sunflower will fit into their gardens. If it is a cottage garden, with a haphazard jumble of plants, the sunflower can be planted anywhere. In more formal gardens it belongs as a backdrop in the border. The sunflower is the perfect choice for the Native American garden, grown with squash, corn, and North American herbs, perfectly at home among its natural companions of bygone centuries.

Melissa officinalis
LEMON BALM

Every age and culture seems to come up with its own version of a life extender—both herbal and otherwise. Two thousand years ago Chinese herbalists lauded homely ginseng as well as the humble peach. Georgian Russian peasants have become well known for their strict diet of yogurt. Mexicans have invested the century plant, or *Agave americana,* with extended-life virtues, inspired by its bizarre habit of sending up twenty-foot flower stalks that bloom every ten years or so in a flourish of giant yellow flowers. And in this century cryogenics as well as a host of products in the classified sections of supermarket tabloids stir the imaginations of those who feel they'll never quite be ready to explore the "Other Side."

In the sixteenth century a Swiss physician revealed in a burst of optimism that lemon balm would most certainly restore new life to those who ingested it. Word spread quickly, and by the next century lemon balm was eagerly cultivated and consumed by would-be eighteenth-centuriates. There are reports in this century of old Britishers who have made a habit of drinking lemon balm tea and breezed past the one-hundred-year mark.

Unlike many herbs that purport to have fabulous medicinal benefits, lemon balm at least cannot harm you. This marvelous little plant, with pretty green leaves that seem to glow with vitality, is still a favorite of herbalists, who recommend taking it as a tea for everything from melancholy to toning the stomach. More importantly, it is a wonderful culinary herb that you will find just the right touch on sorbet or ice cream served in a tall, elegant glass. The leaves have also been

used to bring sprightly taste to vegetable, seafood, and poultry dishes. Simply think of any culinary pairing for mint or lemon and substitute lemon balm in that role.

Those people whose lives are marred by the downside of Type A personalities—either their own or some jumpy companion's—would do well to apply some of their nervous energy to cultivating lemon balm. Although it was prescribed by herbalists in bygone times to stimulate the brain, it has in fact been scientifically proven to have a soporific effect. But one must remember that long ago, before the days of intelligence-quotient testing and other tangible, onerous forms of measuring one's cerebral skills, brain stimulation referred also to calming down the perturbed patient and stirring *up* pleasant thoughts. Such treatments were greatly facilitated by washing herbal medicine *down* with alcohol—a practice still viable today, as it "driveth away heaviness of mind," as one herbalist put it.

In keeping with its relaxed-mood-setting qualities, lemon balm is of easy culture and grows readily from seed in well-drained soil. Although mellow lemon balm prefers sun, it will easily compromise and grow in shade. To preserve its fragrance all year, dry the plant for use in potpourris and sleep pillows, as delightful now as they were centuries ago.

Lemon balm's leaves are citrus scented and minty green, left, betraying its mint family lineage. There are also variegated-leaf forms that look lovely in the garden border. Although the fragrant leaves are most commonly added to potpourris and sachets, the writer John Parkinson believed that this herb was best used in the bath, especially in the summertime, to comfort the "veines and sinewes."

Strawberries à la Haga

Lemon balm is a pleasant departure from the more common practice of garnishing dishes with mint. This tantalizing dessert, shown at right as served at Stallmästaregården in Stockholm, combines the tartness of lemon balm leaves with the sweetness of strawberries and ice cream. This recipe is named for the summer castle of King Gustavus III of Sweden, who ruled in the eighteenth century.

Serves 4

½ cup orange juice
2 tablespoons confectioners' sugar
4 tablespoons Grand Marnier
2 tablespoons grenadine
2 pints strawberries
½ lemon
granulated sugar
1 pint vanilla ice cream
fresh lemon balm leaves
finely shredded orange zest

Mix the orange juice, confectioners' sugar, Grand Marnier, and grenadine together in a large bowl. Slice the strawberries, add to marinade, and marinate them for 1 hour. Run the lemon half around the edges of 4 glasses and dip rims in sugar to coat them. Divide the ice cream and strawberries among the glasses, layering the ingredients to create a striped effect. Garnish with lemon balm leaves and orange zest.

Mentha citrata
LEMON MINT
Mentha requienii
CORSICAN MINT
Mentha spicata
SPEARMINT
Mentha suaveolens
APPLE MINT
Mentha suaveolens Cv.
'Variegata'
PINEAPPLE MINT
Mentha × *gentilis*
GINGER MINT
Mentha × *piperata*
BLACK PEPPERMINT
Mentha × *piperita*
PEPPERMINT

Oscar Wilde once observed, "History is merely gossip," and there are quite a few spicy tales to support this in mint's mythical memoirs. The history of mint reads like a scandal sheet, rife with tales of adultery, hush money, and insobriety.

Mint was named for the nymph Minthē, who was the girlfriend of Pluto, the king of Hades. When Pluto's wife, Persephone, learned of their trysts, she threw Minthē to the ground and trampled on her fragile, unfortunate body. Pluto, who wielded great power in matters pertaining to the afterlife, arranged for her to live on as mint.

This seductively scented herb's reputation did not fare much better in biblical times, when it became sullied by commerce. Aside from being used to pay taxes, mint was often paid to corrupt members of the religious sects as a means of absolving sins and currying worldly favor. The idea of mint as legal tender suggests some connection with the word *mint* in its other usage—a place where coins are made—but that is just a linguistic coincidence, further reinforced by argot expressions such as "mint leaves" for money. As another matter of pure coincidence, plutocrat, a moneyed person, derives from the aforementioned Pluto, another bonding of money and mint.

Stories about mint blow hot and cold. In Grecian times it was believed by some that consuming mint caused impotence. But as the herbalists such as Culpeper later reasoned, because it is an herb governed astrologically by Venus, "it stirreth up venery or bodily lust." John Gerard asserted that smelling mint could provoke another vice, a "greedie desire" for meat.

Mint was later exculpated through an association with the Virgin Mary. In seventeenth-century France spearmint was known as *menthe de Notre Dame,* Our Lady's mint. At around the same time in Italy it came to be known as *erba Santa Maria,* Saint Mary's herb.

But mint's reputation met its undoing again in the New World with the rise of the mint julep. This concoction originated in the American South, and there are many "official" recipes. In its most basic form it involves bourbon, crushed mint leaves, and shaved ice, but the recipe deemed worthy of being recorded in 1848 by Captain Marryat, a British naval officer, called for peach and common brandies as well as fresh pineapple. "I learned how to make them, and succeeded pretty well," he confided to his British readership. And just in case any Britons thought the mint julep might be too much of a hot-weather drink, not suitable for England's brisk climate, he added that it could be enjoyed even when "the thermometer is as low as 70 degrees."

Captain Marryat found the mint julep "irresistible," just the kind of talk that would

Freshly picked spearmint is a refreshing herb to chew on a hot summer day, left. Catnip, bee balm, and purple loosestrife are also part of this late summer harvest. The baby-size leaves of Corsican mint grow happily and securely cradled in a tree trunk, opposite.

sound alarm bells for reform groups such as the Women's Christian Temperance Union. Surely, anything with such a powerful hold on people had to be the devil's handiwork. Temperance crusaders in Virginia in the mid–nineteenth century campaigned for uprooting every bed of mint in the state.

But throughout its history mint has managed to triumph in the kitchen. From ancient times there have always been great believers in mint's virtues, even if it did have unsavory associations. In the only existing cookbook from Greco-Roman times, mint appears frequently. The cookbook was compiled by Marcus Gavius Apicius, a wealthy and no doubt enormously fat man who squandered all his money on banquets. One of Apicius's more memorable recipes calls for boiling ostrich in a stock seasoned with mint. At banquets such as his, the Greeks and Romans also wore this extraordinary herb around their heads for its lovely aroma (and perhaps to chew on between their bibulous, many-coursed meals since it aids digestion). They also infused their sauces and wines with it.

Mint is not exclusive to any one culture, and it is used widely in Europe and the United States. Classic Italian cookery pairs mint with salads and soups (especially with lentils and tomatoes), vegetable and fish dishes. Cooks of the British Isles use mint with lamb, in jellies and sauces, and to accompany cabbage and peas. The settlers in the New World carried on these traditions and dried the leaves so that they could be used in winter for teas. Instead of the heavily sugared, minted chewing gum known today, they offered their children the candied flowers and leaves of mint, which they stored in tightly covered containers to preserve them for winter use.

Mint can be used to even fuller potential today, with so many varieties available to the gardener. The mints that are best known are the spearmint *(Mentha spicata)* and the peppermint *(M. × piperita)*. The former is thought to be one of the elder mints, the one known to ancient

cultures. Its taste is more delicate than that of peppermint and is used principally to flavor foods. It is the *Mentha* of choice for the mint julep but has also been known to flavor candies with its light cool taste.

Peppermint contains menthol, which is extracted from the plant for medicinal and cosmetic uses, such as toothpaste (mints have been used as "toothbrushes" since the Middle Ages). But this versatile herb also brings its pungent-then-cooling flavor to confections, such as after-dinner mints, and to teas and cold summer beverages. It has also been called *brandy mint* because it complements this liquor and is the mint of crème de menthe. The purple-stemmed black peppermints yield the most strongly flavored oil and are most commonly used, although the white types are also valued for their light flavor.

There is confusion about the exact date of peppermint's official debut; it is indigenous to Europe and is a naturally occurring hybrid of spearmint and *M. aquatica,* the wild water mint. Its ancestors might have been known to the ancient Greeks and Romans, but it was in cultivation in England at the end of the seventeenth century and in Europe by the mid–eighteenth century. English peppermint oil has been justifiably famous for centuries for

its pungency and vigor. Peppermint has been cultivated on a commercial scale in Surrey, England, since the eighteenth century. Both peppermint and spearmint were brought to America by the settlers and were grown in great quantity in Colonial dooryard gardens; spearmint has even become naturalized in the American wild.

Many of the other varieties of mints have delightful culinary qualities suggested by their names. Apple mint *(M. suaveolens)* is native to southern and western Europe and has large, cheerful, round leaves with the flavor of minted apples. Botanical nomenclature regarding mint has been revised several times, and this plant has gone by several names, but it seems it has been known by its current name at least since the Victorian era. Try a few sprigs in a hot spiced punch. Pineapple mint, *M. suaveolens* Cv. 'Variegata,' is a cultivar of the apple mint and has an even more complex fruity nature. It would seem to be an excellent mint for Captain Marryat—the mint julep crusader—who liked his julep to have a pineapple undertaste. It has pretty white-and-green variegated leaves, which make it a very dressy garnish. For more fruity notes, try the lemon mint, sometimes also called orange or eau de cologne mint. Use *M. citrata* when you're garnishing food or drinks and would like to add a citrusy taste with a heady aroma. 'Moroccan' mint, a hybrid, will bring an exotic touch to teas and sauces. Corsican mint, *M. requienii,* has tiny, endearing leaves that make a delicate ground cover and filler plant in small spaces. It grows easily between cracks in paving, tucked in tidily like an old lace handkerchief in a pocket. This antique herb also has a lovely, faraway fragrance, similar to peppermint, but also betraying its origins on the balmy Mediterranean island of Corsica. And don't overlook ginger mint *(Mentha × gentilis),* a mint of complex heritage, sweetly scented, and spicy.

The mints' growing habits are in keeping with their history: They tend to become inextricably entangled with things.

This creeping habit will delight you if you want to create a minty ground cover in which the plants grow unchecked. Most mints can be grown from seed; however, you must propagate peppermint from cuttings, layering, or division because it is a sterile hybrid and won't produce seed. Mints, being unusual herbs, also don't grow well in the dry soil that most herbs favor.

Sumac and Mint Cooler

*Why not try this variation on lemonade, using smooth or staghorn sumac berries (*Rhus glabra *and* typhina, *respectively) and mint sprigs? The drink, shown at left, is easy to make and has been recommended by everyone from Euell Gibbons to the cheerful herbalist Pam Montgomery, whose simple recipe should induce you to try making this beverage yourself. Sumac is similar to lemons in its taste and goes down very smoothly. It is a medicinal herb whose leaves and berries were used by the Native Americans to soothe sore throats and bring down fever.*

Makes 1½ cups

1 large cluster of smooth or staghorn sumac
*   berries*
1 fresh mint sprig (lemon mint if
*   available)*
1 pint cold water

Add the berries and mint to the water in a pitcher. Let the mixture sit for 1 hour (it infuses very quickly) in the sun. Cover the top lightly with a small cloth if you wish to keep it pure. Refrigerate and serve icy cold. There's no need to add sugar, but do so if you must.

Variegated-leaf gingermint, opposite, brightens a brick courtyard in a terra-cotta container at Plants from the Past, near the Scottish seaside. This mint has a spicy taste that you can experiment with to alter and update old recipes.

Chef Jane Binns of Rothay Manor in the Cumbria region of England contributes these recipes for an herbal dim-sum-style repast of chicken livers and herbed dip, followed by a minty tart for dessert, shown at left. Oat biscuits are crunchy counterpoints to the dip and fruit and were standard fare in the hilly Cumbria lake district. Served with a fresh salad, this makes a wonderful luncheon and would be complemented by the elder drink recipe on page 81 and the parsley drop scones on page 51.

Marjoram Foies de Poulet

A novel way to serve chicken livers (rich in vitamins A and B) is with herbs. Children can be induced to eat this healthy food when it is dressed up with marjoram and cream. Or you can tell them, as the ancients believed, that eating livers can allow one to divine the future.

Serves 3 to 4

1 pound chicken livers
¼ cup unsalted butter
½ onion, coarsely chopped
2 cups chicken stock
2 teaspoons minced fresh marjoram
1 cup heavy cream
¼ cup all-purpose flour, seasoned with salt and pepper
1 tablespoon chopped fresh parsley
selection of vegetables (peppers, chives, carrots, celery), julienned and blanched, for garnish

Trim livers. In 2-quart saucepan, over medium heat, melt 1 tablespoon butter. Cook trimmings and onions until golden. Add stock, reduce heat to medium low, and simmer for 45 minutes.

Strain stock through 2 to 3 layers of cheesecloth; bring to a boil, and boil for 10 minutes to reduce. Add marjoram and cream and reduce heat to medium and cook until the sauce coats the back of a spoon. Adjust seasoning to taste and keep warm.

Dust livers lightly with seasoned flour and sauté in 10-inch skillet with remaining butter for 5 minutes on each side; livers should be pink in the center.

Place cooked livers on a serving platter. Coat with the sauce, sprinkle with parsley, and garnish with a julienne of blanched vegetables.

Herbed Dip with Fresh Fruit

Here is a fresh alternative to packaged snack foods.

Serves 3 to 4

6 tablespoons unsalted butter
1 cup full-fat cream cheese
1 clove garlic, crushed
½ teaspoon each chopped fresh parsley, sage, thyme, tarragon, chervil, chives, and winter savory
Kiwifruit, oranges, peaches, strawberries, and pineapple

Melt butter and cool. Place cream cheese in a food processor or blender and slowly mix in butter, crushed garlic, and chopped herbs.

Spoon or pipe the dip from a pastry bag with a ¼-inch tip into small pots and serve with a selection of fresh fruits. Serve with oat biscuits or fresh rolls.

Mint Tart

Pâte sucrée is a sweet pastry dough. In this beautiful mint dessert, it lends itself perfectly to the crisp taste of mint.

Serves 8 to 10

pâte sucrée (recipe follows)
1 cup dried currants
6 tablespoons unsalted butter, melted
2 tablespoons chopped candied orange peel
6 large fresh mint sprigs, chopped (reserve 8 whole leaves for garnish)
3 tablespoons golden syrup (available in specialty food stores)
2 tablespoons turbinado sugar (substitute white sugar if unavailable)
½ cup heavy cream, whipped (for garnish)

Prepare the pâte sucrée.

In small bowl, soak the currants in 1 cup boiling water or fruit juice for at least 1 hour to plump them up. (It's best to let them soak overnight.) Drain currants.

Preheat the oven to 325 degrees Fahrenheit. Roll out three quarters of the pâte sucrée and press into an 8- to 10-inch tart pan, allowing for a ½-inch overhang. Brush with a bit of melted butter. Fill with drained currants and orange peel and sprinkle with chopped mint. Pour golden syrup and remaining melted butter on top.

Roll out remaining pastry and cut into ¼-inch strips. Top the tart with pastry strips placed diagonally to form a latticework pattern. Pinch the ends of the pastry strips and the overhanging bottom crust together. Trim off excess pastry from outside of pan edge. Brush pastry with cold water and sprinkle with sugar. Bake for 25 to 30 minutes, until lightly browned. Let cool.

Pâte Sucrée

2 cups flour
2 tablespoons sugar
¼ teaspoon salt
½ cup cold butter, cut into small pieces
¼ cup vegetable shortening
4-6 tablespoons ice water

Mix flour, sugar, and salt in a medium bowl. Add butter and shortening and work into flour with a pastry blender, or two knives used scissor fashion, until mixture has the consistency of oatmeal. Add water, one tablespoon at a time, until the dough holds together in a ball. Put dough on a lightly floured surface and smear it, several tablespoons at a time, across the surface to mix the fat and flour. Scrape up the dough and knead it very briefly into a smooth ball. Refrigerate at least two hours before rolling out.

Ocimum basilicum
AROMATIC BASIL
Ocimum sanctum
SACRED BASIL

When Alexander the Great ascended the throne of Macedonia at age twenty-one in 336 B.C., soon after completing his formal education with his tutor, Aristotle, his thoughts were not unlike those of any modern economics or political science major just graduated from college and looking to put his mark on the world. Alexander began his campaign for power by gaining ascendancy over Greece, squelching uprisings and sacking cities when necessary. The ambitious Alexander succeeded in defeating the Persians and then dashed ahead into Egypt, where he established a city named for himself: Alexandria.

Then, having won control of the ancient world, Alexander turned to more serious, intellectual pursuits. By age twenty-six he had lived more fully than most people do in a lifetime. Now, in his old age (at least relative to the thirty-three total years of his life), he was more of a graduate school type. He continued to indulge his addiction for conquering but partially split his discipline by studying botany.

To embark on this challenging new project, he naturally turned to the greatest intellectual he knew, his old tutor, Aristotle. Alexander asked Aristotle to help him out by writing an account of a mission to India in which a trained team of men would take notes on plants and animals and send these back to the old sage. Among the plants Alexander and his men encountered and felt worthy of recording back home was a particularly outstanding plant with sleek leaves and a deliciously spicy scent—aromatic basil, *Ocimum basilicum.* It is believed that Alexander was so impressed by basil that he sent back seeds as well, since the plant is recorded as having grown in ancient Greece. This is generally accepted as the explanation how the plant first came to be grown there.

Aristotle had agreed to Alexander's plan, but like many great minds he was completely inept at ever really completing what he had started. Most of his writings are the results of his students' copious note-taking. True to form, Aristotle only scrawled down notes on the mission's findings. After Alexander's death in 323 B.C., there were uprisings in Athens that prompted Aristotle to flee the city. After Aristotle's death it fell to Theophrastus, another of his students, to tidy up the project and make sense of the notes. Theophrastus used these extensively in the *History of Plants,* which was published under his own name.

Thus basil made its long journey from its native India, where it has been revered for centuries. From Greece, of course, it spread throughout Europe, finding a particularly receptive and enthusiastic audience in Italy, the country with which it has become identified. The association of basil with Alexander, his untimely death, and the bloody uprisings of the day might actually be the key to basil's reputation and centuries-old linkage with evil.

Before Theophrastus had had a chance to organize Aristotle's text, basil had widely entered Grecian culture and had become a staple of the kitchen garden. But while it was considered a potent love charm, it had also gained the reputation of "devil plant." The belief also arose that the plant would not flourish unless the gardener hurled profuse (and unprintable) insults at it during planting. Theophrastus, a levelheaded man, quickly pronounced this nonsense and tried to head off the ridiculous rumors before they became entrenched in popular culture.

But it was too late. Along with much Hellenistic culture, the belief was absorbed readily into Roman life. Pliny the Elder reports the same practice of cursing the plant in ancient Rome and also the use of it as a love charm. To add to the confusion, the plant's old Greek name, *basilikos* (which means royalty, probably in connection with its original revered status in India), got mixed up with the Latin *basiliscus* (meaning basilisk, an evil, dragonlike legendary animal), which could kill simply by looking at you or breathing on you; various beliefs in ensuing centuries asserted that the plant could protect you from the basilisk or, under different circumstances, could actually breed such a beast. The result was that basil, so wonderful to eat but so mystical in origin, became simultaneously feared and revered, with much the same spirit that the Japanese eat the notorious delicacy fugu today.

At some less-celebrated point, sacred basil *(O. sanctum),* also made a journey from India to the Continent. In the Hindu religion this extremely aromatic, nonculinary plant is known as holy or sacred herb and is thought to be a favorite plant of both Vishnu and Krishna.

Unfortunately, basil became even more strongly associated with death as a result of Giovanni Boccaccio's wildly popular *Decameron,* a fourteenth-century collection of one hundred tales spiced with details of everyday life. Basil, such a classic quotidian Italian herb, was included in the story of a young girl who nurtured her basil plants with the corpse of her dead lover, Lorenzo, as well as her own tears. This story is particularly shocking when one considers that in Italy a woman traditionally signifies her willingness to receive a male guest by placing a pot of basil outside her door! A similar but racier use of basil in modern Spain is deliberately kept quiet. An itinerant artist friend who lived in Majorca reveals

A bevy of basils grows happily together at the Well-Sweep Herb Farm in New Jersey, opposite. Sacred basil grows in the left rear, with cinnamon basil, purple basil, Tulsi green basil, miniature purple basil, Armenian basil, and little-leaf basil all present as well.

that pots of basil on windows and balconies signify a house of ill repute.

Don't let basil's checkered associations deter you from planting this fragrant, vibrant plant, and you need not settle for just the green ovate leafy form in your garden. There are so many varieties of basil derived from ancient *O. basilicum* available today, from so many different regions, that it's almost possible to create a garden varied in texture and color using only this plant. There's the purple ruffles type (*O. basilicum* 'Purple Ruffles'), wonderful for salads and pesto. Along with dark opal basil (*O. basilicum* 'Purparescens'), it will create a section of deep-reddish-toned garden color. The cinnamon basil (*O. basilicum* 'Cinnamon') has the spicy overtones its name implies and brings sprightly taste to sorbets and iced drinks. The lettuce-leaf basil (*O. basilicum* 'Green Ruffles') outperforms most greens in salads. Or simply use basic aromatic basil in one of the oldest recorded usages of the plant as a culinary herb, as did Apicius—the portly party-giver of ancient Rome—as a flavoring for peas, cooked in a bit of wine.

Sea Bass with Summer Vegetables

Basil is a remarkably versatile culinary herb. Used here by Chef David Goode of Cannizaro House in London, it combines flavorfully with an old cohort, wine. A favorite dish of ancient Rome was basil, wine, and other herbs used to season peas. Here the two make an excellent complement to sea bass, shown at right.

Serves 2

¾ pound sea bass fillet
1 cup fish stock
½ cup dry white wine
1 shallot, minced
½ bunch fresh basil leaves, chopped (reserve a few leaves for garnish)
½ cup heavy cream
¼ cup cold unsalted butter, cut into small pieces
salt and pepper to taste
1 carrot, julienned
½ leek, julienned
2 stalks celery, julienned
dried seaweed for garnish

In large sauté pan, over medium high heat, poach sea bass in fish stock and white wine, 10 to 12 minutes, until sea bass is almost done. Remove it from pan and cover with buttered wax paper to keep it moist and hot. Reserve liquid.

In 2-quart saucepan, sauté the shallot and basil in 2 tablespoons butter for five minutes. Add reserved cooking liquid; bring to a boil; reduce by half. Add heavy cream; reduce heat to medium high and cook to reduce by half. The mixture should thickly coat a spoon and slowly drip off. Whisk in remaining butter to add glaze to sauce. Season to taste. Keep warm.

In a third saucepan, blanch vegetables for about a minute in salted boiling water. Refresh with cold water and drain.

Remove paper from fish and place fish on a serving plate. Coat fish with sauce and garnish with the julienne of vegetables and crumbled seaweed.

Focaccia with Yogurt Cheese and Herbs

Fresh ingredients make even the humblest meal taste exceptional. Wendy and Michael London of Rock Hill Bakehouse in upstate New York apply this philosophy not only to their breads but also to their family meals. Fresh herbs from their garden and yogurt prepared on the premises make this focaccia especially wonderful and a real treat for their daughter, Sophie, who is shown patiently awaiting her slice, opposite page. Wendy London stresses that the cook should create any mix of herbs desired in this recipe. One flavor can predominate, or the herbs can be mixed, depending on personal taste.

Makes one 9- to 10-inch-diameter focaccia

2 cloves garlic
⅓ cup chopped fresh herbs (basil, parsley, thyme, oregano, rosemary, or sage, in any proportion)
3 tablespoons olive oil
1 cup yogurt cream cheese (recipe follows)
pinch salt
focaccia dough (recipe follows)
4 basil leaves for garnish

Preheat oven to 450 degrees Fahrenheit. Chop garlic and herbs together. In a small bowl, mix together garlic, herbs, and olive oil to make a thick mixture; and mix in yogurt cream cheese. Add salt. Spread on unbaked dough. Bake for 15 to 25 minutes, until dough is golden brown. Garnish with basil leaves. Serve warm.

Yogurt Cream Cheese

1 quart yogurt (non-homogenized is best)

Place yogurt in cheesecloth gathered together and tied in a colander over a large bowl. Strain out excess liquid after 15 minutes; refrigerate overnight. It should have the consistency of homemade cream cheese, which is looser than the commercial kind. Drain liquid and use in pancakes or the like. Store cheese in crock or container. It keeps for 1 week or longer if made into patties and stored in jar of virgin olive oil.

Focaccia Dough

1 cup cool water
2 tablespoons olive oil
¾ teaspoon sea salt
2¾ cups unbleached bread flour
scant ¼ ounce fresh yeast cake

In a large bowl, stir together water, olive oil, and salt before adding flour and fresh cake yeast (add as you would any dry ingredient).

Mix until the dough mass no longer sticks to the bowl (some additional flour may have to be added). Turn out onto a lightly floured surface and knead for 10 minutes.

Coat the inside of a large bowl with olive oil. Place dough in the bowl and turn over to coat all sides with oil. Cover with a cloth, and allow to stand until double its size, about 2½ hours.

Punch dough down and shape into a 9- to 10-inch round with fingers. You may, however, refrigerate this dough overnight before shaping. The additional slow fermentation will improve the flavor and makes the dough easier to handle.

Rosmarinus officinalis
ROSEMARY

In the fifteenth century, when much of the world was still being mapped, no mariner dared sail beyond the western coast of Africa. Dead seamen's souls might attack ships passing through; terrible monsters resided in the environs. Beyond what we now call Cape Verde, it was believed, there lay the Sea of Darkness—surely the end of the road for the mariner.

But Prince Henry the Navigator of Portugal believed otherwise and was determined to claim the land beyond the "end of the world" for his country. Of course, he could afford to be brave, sitting on his throne in sunny Portugal and idly tinkering with maps. After sending fifteen successive ships on the journey, in 1434 he induced Gil Eanes to lead a mission that would circle the cape—no matter what happened.

Eanes went along with the plan and somehow forced his crewmen to steer the ship around the cape. When they rounded it, the waters were calm, no monsters arose from the depths, no spiny hands clutched from the water. It was pleasant, so they continued sailing—but still with some apprehension. After sailing a bit more near the coastline, they spotted (and no doubt smelled) a familiar bluish-green plant. Excited, they pulled up on shore and confirmed their hopes: it was rosemary. They gathered the plant and brought it home.

Rosemary, long a form of protection against evil, confirmed Prince Henry's belief that the world beyond the cape was a benevolent place. And after its discovery in

A carpet of interwoven dwarf hyssop, barberry, lavender, and germander spreads out at the feet of a rosemary candelabrum, above. The rosemary topiary is flanked by sculpted lemon verbena.

Africa, it wasn't so difficult to induce others to make the trip and finish mapping the African coastline.

Rosemary has always held a place of esteem. The plant was a daily feature of Grecian life. Students braided it in their hair because they thought the fragrance would help them remember facts for important tests. It then became associated with remembrance—as Shakespeare reminds us with the line in *Hamlet,* "There's rosemary, that's for remembrance."

The plant was frequently added to brides' bouquets to symbolize that they remembered the love of their paternal homes and would carry that spirit on to the next. The bridegroom, too, did not forget his rosemary. Friends of the bride would make a nosegay bound with golden ribbon or lace for him as a reminder that he should be faithful. Up until the nineteenth century this plant was also tossed on coffins in funeral rites to signify remembrance of the dead.

It seems odd that such customs should have died out, since they persisted for so many centuries and are really very charming. But rosemary has in general lost its prominence in everyday life. Once the most illustrious herb of all, rosemary now is relegated to the kitchen, where it is not used often enough.

Those who wish to grow rosemary will be astounded by the range of types. Rosemary's range of flower colors is also impressive, as you might select a tender or bold blue, pure white, or pink. There are prostrate types that act as pretty, fragrant ground covers, as well as upright growers that can be left to spread shrubbily or be coaxed into shapes. People who live in climates where the temperatures drop considerably in winter find that they must bring rosemary indoors for the cold spells, and one method of enjoying rosemary indoors is the trained standard. The plant is coaxed through clipping and staking into special forms to make a charming centerpiece.

Roast Rack of Lamb with Rosemary and Mint

This flavorful dish, created by Chef Colin Warwick of Prestonfield House in Edinburgh, Scotland, requires only a light sauce to coat the lamb because the herbs provide so much flavor. Chef Warwick serves the dish, shown below, with a side dish of shoestring potatoes, or "straw chips," as they are known in Scotland.

Serves 2

Mint Hollandaise

2 fresh mint sprigs (use stems and leaves for reduction; reserve 4 leaves for garnish)
8 peppercorns, crushed
6 tablespoons white wine vinegar
3 egg yolks
½ cup unsalted butter, melted

1 frenched rack of lamb, seasoned with salt and pepper to taste
1 clove garlic, cut into thin slivers
3 fresh rosemary sprigs cut into 2-inch lengths
2 large tomatoes

Preheat oven to 425 degrees Fahrenheit. Mix mint, peppercorns, and wine vinegar in 1-quart saucepan; boil over medium high heat until reduced by half. Strain through cheesecloth into small bowl and cool.

Make small slits all over the lamb with the point of a small knife and insert garlic. Split the lamb in several places between the bones and also insert sprigs of rosemary.

Roast lamb quickly, for 8 to 10 minutes, and leave pink. (Meat thermometer reads 140° for rare, 165° for medium, 170° to 180° Fahrenheit for well done.) Just at the end of the roasting, add some extra rosemary to roast and turn joint around, taking care not to scorch herbs. Lift lamb out. Drain off fat, boil drippings to reduce, and strain. (Thicken the gravy if desired.) Keep warm and serve in sauceboat.

Reduce heat to 300 degrees Fahrenheit. Slice off the top ½ inch of the tomatoes and scoop out the flesh, leaving a firm shell. Warm the tomatoes in a shallow pan for about 5 minutes.

While tomatoes are cooking, make the hollandaise. Place yolks and 2 tablespoons strained reduction in double boiler and cook over hot water (not boiling). Whisk until the whisk leaves a trace in the yolk mixture. Remove from heat and whisk in butter gradually. Check seasoning for salt and pepper. Makes about ⅔ cup of sauce. Keep sauce warm.

When the tomatoes are warm, pour mint hollandaise into them and garnish with the reserved mint leaves.

Salvia officinalis
COMMON SAGE
Salvia sclarea
CLARY SAGE

Before the days of organized feminism, women asserted themselves in more subtle ways than suffragette marches. There is an old British folkloric belief that sage flourishes in gardens where the woman runs the household, and this would explain, at least partially, why sage was so assiduously cultivated by the cottager wife from medieval times up until the Victorian era. One can easily imagine the self-satisfaction on a countrywoman's face when sage flourished in her garden.

And what subjugated husband could complain about the public display of his wife's domestic sway, when it meant he could feast on such savory dishes as duck with sage and onion stuffing, herbed sage cheese, meat pie with sage, and stews richly flavored with a potent *bouquet garni* of sage, thyme, and marjoram? Any smart second-fiddle spouse would accept his fate quietly in exchange for such palatable cures as a glass of medicinal sage wine or a warming cup of sage tea.

In administering such treatments, the housewife was merely following in a tradition of using sage that extends back to antiquity. No other herb could be more appropriately linked to women. Based on the writings of Hippocrates, Dioscorides, and Galen (Marcus Aurelius's doctor), Roman physicians used the herb to treat various female maladies as well as to confer long life. This gentle herb, empathetic to human needs, was the darling of the herbal scribes of antiquity. The ancient Greeks made an annual ritual of

offering it to the mythological figure Cadmus, who was credited with discovering the healing properties of sage. Perhaps it was sage that provided his vigor for his other heroic feats: founding the city of Thebes and killing the sacred dragon that guarded the spring of Ares, the god of war.

Dioscorides provided a detailed recipe for a medicinal sage wine that would take only three months to ferment. He recommended this beverage for all sorts of bodily complaints, among them ulcers, spleen difficulty, and dysentery. Later the Roman writer Pliny the Elder commented that it was an excellent wound herb for stingray and snake bites. The Romans conferred on it its genus name, *Salvia,* which is derived from the Latin word *salvere,* "to be in good health."

Sage's popularity and exceptional reputation extend across cultural borders. The druids of ancient Celtic Britain had their own procedure involving sage. When they weren't offering human sacrifices to nature gods in oak groves, they were trying to produce the very opposite effect: resuscitating the dead using sage. Such was their belief in its healing powers. And it has long been an Arabic belief that sage is brain food and ingesting it can actually increase your intelligence. In tenth-century Italy the

medical school at Salerno gave its students an easy-to-remember cure-all prescription: *Cur morietur homo cui salvia crescit in horto?* or "Why should a man die when sage grows in his garden?"

There are more than seven hundred species of sage. Wherever they grow, these aromatic plants infuse the air with a magical scent thought to induce sleep. There are varieties of sage native to such diverse locales as the Canary Islands, the United States, the Middle East, Europe, and South America. Their astonishing variety of forms encompass the spiny, woolly-leaved thistle sage of California, the scarlet-flowered sage of Brazil, and the silver sage of southern Europe, with gorgeous pastel petals.

But relatively few of the sages have herbal usages, and the one that has stirred up most of the ancient enthusiasm is *Salvia officinalis,* culinary sage. In his *Herball or Generall Historie of Plantes,* John Gerard proudly revealed that he cultivated this classic herb garden plant, native to the Mediterranean, in several forms, red (which was once thought to divine the future if steeped in rose water on Midsummer Eve) and variegated-leaf among them. Gerard, however, would have been more concerned with the medicinal than the culinary aspects of the plant. This tradition extended even to North America: approximately two centuries later the Shakers used culinary sage medicinally to produce night sweats, cure coughs and colds, and expel worms.

The leaves of culinary sage are still used by herbalists as an astringent and as an antiseptic to treat wounds or to soothe sore throats. But, as the common name suggests, culinary sage is most often put to use today in the kitchen. Sage leaves are lovely blended with cream cheese and spread on delicate tea sandwiches, a practice that is

The muted greens of common sage contrast strikingly with bright nasturtiums, above. In a Scandinavian island garden, opposite, purple-blue sage flowers grow near hops—once used to relieve ear- and toothache—trained up poles.

seen more in Europe than in the United States. Culinary sage leaves are interesting salad ingredients, can be added to soups and breads, and are delicious when added to a breading for fish. When culinary sage is added to stuffing, the effect is beyond comparison to the dusty bread crumb varieties that are so often served.

A more unusual sage, probably not known to the ancient Greeks and Romans but enthusiastically written up in the great age of herbals, is clary. It would certainly have been one of the herbs of choice for the impregnable medieval wife; it is such a showy, spectacular plant that it cannot help drawing admiring glances. Resembling delicate Oriental papercraft, clary's violet, white, or blue flowers are arranged in cuplike whorls on spires complemented by downy heart-shaped leaves.

Clary goes by many names. It makes such a good visual impression that medieval doctors did not hesitate to prescribe it for people with eye trouble. Because simmering the seeds in water produces a sticky decoction, they reasoned that this stickiness would be an excellent agent to place in the eyes to remove foreign matter. Its species name and common names are the result of a hybridizing of Old English, Middle English, and Latin. They mean "clear," inspired by the practice of clearing out the eye. Clary's eye-soothing reputation also inspired another one of its antique names, *Oculus Christi,* or Christ's-eye.

You've probably sampled clary unknowingly when eating candies or baked goods, or perhaps you've had a hint of clary's fragrance in your cologne or soap, as an aromatic oil distilled from the plants is used in flavorings and perfumery. Still, this ancient ingredient deserves to be used more prominently. Clary flowers are a beautiful garnish, and the flowers as well as the leaves produce a soothing tea.

The leaves of clary can be used in the same manner as culinary sage. You may find the eighteenth-century practice of using them in omelets especially to your liking. It

was once thought in England that such a concoction would help cure back problems. The American colonists used clary as a vegetable, adding the leaves to salads or cooking and eating them as a side dish, and in winter they used dried leaves for tea. The flowers are perfect for sachets and potpourri.

If you feel inspired to cultivate sages, plant them where there is good soil drainage and plenty of sun. It is critical—especially if you are a married woman—to keep the soil from becoming too moist; otherwise root rot could occur and cause your sages to founder. Common sage grows to about two feet, and clary stretches even higher, to three feet or more.

Sambucus nigra EUROPEAN ELDER
Sambucus canadensis AMERICAN ELDER

John Parkinson's compact locution to describe the herb, "for use or delight," could hardly apply more completely to any other plant than the elder. For those who feel that they have to choose between beauty and utility when planting an herb garden, the elder is a wonderful discovery. In the aristocracy of the herbal world the elder ranks at least among the *noblesse ancienne*. This beautiful shrub, with tender, feathery, creamy white blossoms that appear in June and July, deserves a place of supremacy in the herb garden.

In its long history of herbal applications every part of the elder has been used medicinally. In medieval Europe the root juice and bark were used as a purgative and body cleanser. These "tonics," however, must have left their patients somewhat shaken: the plant contains cyanide! The Shakers enthusiastically used the American elder, *Sambucus canadensis,* medicinally, employing the bark for dropsy (an archaic term for edema), for bringing down fevers, and as a general tonic—known in their herbal terminology as an "alterative"—to set the body straight. Elder-flower water was popular among Victorian ladies, who dabbed it on to soothe and lighten their skin.

With the exception of elder-flower water, none of the aforementioned medicinal usages are recommended for the casual herb gardener today, as there is insufficient evidence to support the validity of these "cures." But don't despair. There are safe herbal applications for the elder, aside, of course, from feasting on its cooked berries. The flowers of the elder, known as elder blow, are among the culinary herbs, and they are sheer heaven when stewed with fruit, especially gooseberries.

It is unclear when elder first came to be enjoyed simply as food. Henry V, who reigned in fifteenth-century England, was said very much to enjoy eating the flowers, no doubt after they had been steeped in wine. Today they are fried up as fritters and made into wine in Appalachia. Scandinavians enjoy elder flowers in a midsummer drink. Elder flowers are also used in making tea, sometimes combined with mint.

Although there is truth to the medicinal benefits of elder-flower tea, it was believed that the elder cured through its magical abilities rather than its vitamin content. And for the elder to work its magic, it did not have to be ingested. Residents of Yorkshire, England, once believed that the elder could

European elder trees, below, are rarely felled by superstitious farmers, who believe that the trees have otherworldly powers. The rustic-looking shrub is also deliberately cultivated in the home garden, opposite.

divine the future: they used elder wood in an incantation to ascertain whether livestock was dying as a result of a witch's spell. And throughout Britain it was once believed that the stems or branches of the elder if fashioned into a necklace could magically calm babies. If the plant were growing out of a tree stump, it would be especially rife with magical powers. In many northern European countries a quaint practice was to tip your hat to the elder as you passed it. Perhaps this odd rite came about because of the long-standing belief that Christ's cross was fashioned from elder wood.

The elder is one of the principal powerful Scandinavian flowers of midsummer. Danes once believed that the Midsummer Eve reveler who stood under the elder tree at midnight would be able to spot the fairy leader and his band of servants passing through the countryside.

Superstitious Danes once also feared a spirit thought to live in the elder called Hyldemör, or Elder-Mother. This mysterious woman guarded the sacred elder, bringing harm to anyone who damaged it. If a peasant absolutely had to cut down an elder, he knew that he must first beg the shrub's permission and then, if the tree did not respond in some negative way to the request—presumably by flailing the inquisitor with its branches—the peasant would spit three times before cutting. To this day, great stands of elder still cover many farmers' fields in Scandinavia, a tribute either to the peasants' faint hearts or to the plant's imposing reputation.

But perhaps the farmers simply value the beauty of the elder. These lovely shrubs grow to the size of trees, twenty or twenty-five feet high, and impart a casual, unstudied grace to their surroundings. Adding an elder to your garden will give it a rustic air. The European elder and the American elder alike benefit from moist soil. Give them ample space to spread out and maybe even add a bench beneath the shrubs so that you can relax in their flowery shade in summer.

Elder-Flower Sherbert

This Swedish version of Italian ice uses all-natural ingredients. Simply use the Midsummer Eve Elder Blossom Nectar recipe (opposite page) as a basis. Champagne can also be added to make a frozen herbal drink for special occasions, as is done at Stallmästaregården, Stockholm.

1½ quarts Midsummer Eve Elder Blossom
    Nectar
6 tablespoons lemon juice
2 tablespoons sugar
½ tablespoon gelatine dissolved in 2
    tablespoons warm water

In large bowl mix all ingredients together and freeze in an ice-cream maker according to manufacturer's directions.

Elder flowers have an appetizing scent that suggests their culinary uses, below. They have been combined with rhubarb in jams, made into syrups and teas, and are even an ingredient in wine, as are their famous berries.

Midsummer Eve Elder Blossom Nectar

Elder grows abundantly in the province of Skåne, Sweden's lake district. Scandinavians drink it alone for refreshment or add vodka and white wine, especially to celebrate midsummer. Pernilla Fredriksson, a resident of Skåne, makes the drink with a preservative and times the preparation of her beverage to coincide with Midsummer Eve. She begins to make it on June 16 and lets its flavor intensify for a week so that it will be ready for June 23. Eva Falck, another Skåne resident, who runs Tirup's Örtagård, makes the mixture

without preservatives (as presented here) and serves it immediately, as shown above. She recommends freezing the mixture in plastic containers or as ice cubes so that the beverage can be enjoyed year-round. Simply remove the frozen mixture from the freezer, place the container in a tub of warm water when you want to defrost it, and use it in drinks throughout the winter. She also points out that elder flowers can be frozen—stored loosely in plastic bags filled with some air—and be made into a drink at a later date.

Makes about 3 quarts

50 elder blossoms
4 pounds white or brown sugar
2 lemons, sliced
2 ounces ascorbic acid crystals (about ¼ cup)
2 quarts boiling water

Wash blossoms in cold water. Place blossoms, sugar, lemons, and ascorbic acid in a large metal container. Add boiling water and stir.

Refrigerate mixture for a week, stirring once daily. Strain through cheesecloth and store in clean glass bottles in refrigerator. It will keep for about a week.

Thymus serpyllum
CREEPING THYME
MOTHER-OF-THYME
Thymus vulgaris
CULINARY THYME

Pungent, aromatic thyme is the cornerstone of the herb garden, providing a scented, tufted carpet and even nestling into chinks in garden walls. This rural plant is a favorite of serious gardeners who demand more than looks and charming histories from their herbs, for thyme serves them well both in the kitchen—as a complement to poultry, fish, lamb, beef, and a great number of vegetables—and as a fragrant garden plant.

It is easy to imagine how thyme became associated early in its history with a mystical, unseen dimension; its spicy, sometimes citrusy perfume would seem a likely conduit to the spirit world and is so intense it was believed that it could temporarily capture the attention of divine spirits and make it possible to communicate with them. For this purpose thyme was burned as an offering to the gods (and as an insect repellent) by superstitious thyme-scent fanatics of ancient Greece. The genus name is thought to be derived from a Greek word meaning to fumigate; but the pleasant scent of thyme was probably all the excuse ever needed to set it aflame.

This practice of having thyme to burn (the English poet William Shenstone called the plant "pun-provoking thyme") later continued in Algeria, Morocco, and anywhere else where people could think of an excuse to kindle a thyme fire. People would gather on Midsummer Day for thyme burning, thrilling to the great billows of magically scented smoke spiraling upward in honor of

the vegetation god—an atmosphere not unlike the pyrotechnic displays of today. Although you probably don't want to set your thyme aflame, you might want to update an old Bohemian practice of fumigating a Christmas tree with thyme. Instead of burning the plant, simply deck the tree with dried sprigs harvested in summer or fresh ones if you grow thyme indoors.

Thyme has an enchanted look about it, and in medieval England a belief sprang up that fairies dwelt among banks of thyme. There was even a potion in Renaissance times that called for ingesting thyme: the potion could help you see these fairies while also protecting you from their mischief. Shakespeare drew on such beliefs in *A Midsummer-Night's Dream,* in which Oberon, the King of the Fairies, says, "I

know a bank where the wild thyme blows / Where oxlips and the nodding violet grows."

Some people speculate that Shakespeare might have visited the celebrated herbalist John Gerard's London garden and inspected the many herbs, including thymes, which Gerard grew there. There is even some evidence that the great herbalist and the great bard lived around the corner from each other at one point. Gerard devoted a great deal of space in his writings to thyme, taking pains to distinguish between the "wilde" and "garden" types. He

Leaves and flowers of culinary thyme have long been prized to season foods, above. Creeping thyme brings an enchanting air to a Scottish herb garden visited by bees and gnomes, opposite.

felt that both had numerous medicinal usages, but the former (*T. serpyllum,* creeping thyme) "helpeth the Lethargie, frensie and madness" and the latter (*T. vulgaris,* culinary thyme) was more effective for treating common coughs and plain old melancholy. Oberon might have found either type useful.

Much confusion surrounds the naming and classifying of thyme. *Thymus* is a botanical muddle involving as many as four hundred species, all swarming in confused order in the horticultural encyclopedia. To preserve one's sanity it would be well to remember that common thyme is the ancient thyme grown in the kitchen or herb garden

as a culinary herb. All other thyme species are wonderful for ornament and scent and efficient for attracting bees; think of these as household herbs. Of course, many people have used the creeping types for culinary purposes and medicinal teas. However, the names get switched about so much that one person's creeping lemon thyme is another's lemon barona thyme, and you should consult local sources regarding how to put your creepers to use.

Taken on its own, creeping thyme might not be impressive, but let it spread out and interweave with other creepers with different-colored flowers, and a pastiche results that is as complex as any antique

quilt or Oriental carpet. The creeping thymes inspired John Evelyn, a seventeenth-century English writer, to suggest that such thymes might be employed to add a pleasant fragrance to the London air—a thought that still sounds appealing to urban dwellers, whose lives would be greatly improved if beds of thyme sprang up to cushion hard sidewalks and to perfume alleyways with lemony, minty, pine, fruity, and even spicy scents. These are the thymes with which to create a fragrance garden; harvest them to create delicate sachets, perhaps mixed with mints, scented-geranium leaves, roses, and other deliciously scented plants.

Tropaeolum majus
NASTURTIUM

Cityfolk recently transplanted to the country would do well to plant nasturtium as soon as the weather allows. Metropolitan friends will inevitably want to see how you're faring in the boondocks, and you need to take action to demonstrate your rural skills. Nasturtium, a bright, pleasant culinary herb, will make you look not only like a wonderful gardener but also a competent country cook.

Nasturtium grows so easily in average soil in a good sunny spot that it would be extremely difficult to inhibit the healthy growth of this annual vinelike plant. From seeds sown in spring come flowers that bloom all summer long, so no matter when guests arrive, and no matter how many other difficult flowers droop and herbs sulk, the cheerful nasturtium will be continuously in full flower. Its broad funnel-shaped flowers and lovely segmented leaves, which resemble lily pads or warriors' shields, will cause your guests to gasp with wonder at your horticultural prowess.

In the late afternoon, as you stroll through the garden with your guests, they may remark on the vivid coloration of the nasturtium. Be sure to plant them in a variety of colors—canary yellow, pumpkin, and scarlet—to create the rainbow look of a South American textile, in commemoration of the plants' ancestral home.

Later, as you sit down for a meal with your guests, your salad of nasturtium flowers and leaves, mixed with other wonderful

Nasturtium is truly a Renaissance herb, right. It captured the European imagination during that era, and it can do all things well. Beautifully scented in the garden, it is tasty on the plate, too.

greens from your herb garden, will impress them with its smooth, peppery tastes. Keep in mind that people who have subsisted on frozen vegetables and dried packaged condiments are uninitiated to many edible flowers' charms, so your guests may at first be wary of the nasturtium flower sitting so pertly in the middle of their plates. Once they have tasted it, though, even the most confirmed city slicker will pronounce the nasturtium delicious.

You will further amaze your guests with your herbal knowledge when you reveal that eating nasturtiums is certainly nothing new. The conquistadores brought them to Spain in the sixteenth century, and they were soon known all over Europe. In North America in the seventeenth century, flowers were gathered for bouquets, and the blossoms and leaves were eaten in salads.

If you have your meal outdoors, schedule it near dusk and advise your guests to watch for flashes of light emanating from the flowers just as the sun sets. This was a popular practice in Europe and the United States for centuries. (Even the perfectly sane wife of the Swedish botanist Carl Linnaeus reportedly observed the phenomenon.) The flashes could be explained as an optical illusion, as so many people have claimed to see it happen with other yellow and orange flowers, such as calendula or pot marigold.

From there your casual discussion of the nasturtium can easily expand to discuss the origin of the flower's name. Warn your guests not to confuse the South American plant with the true nasturtium, *Nasturtium officinale*, or watercress, a European plant of an entirely different genus, which nevertheless it greatly resembles. Advise them also not to mistake nasturtium for *Capparis spinosa*, the true caper. The latter mistake could be made by confusing the true caper with the nasturtium's "capers," which are simply the flower buds pickled in vinegar—a usage that dates back to the days of the Colonial American housewife, who had to substitute and innovate to keep her family's lifestyle up to par.

When your guests depart, give them a nasturtium bouquet—the plants flower so prolifically that you will have more blossoms the next day.

Wild Herb Salad

Susun Weed, herbalist of Woodstock, New York, believes, true to her name, that wild plants are underutilized as food sources. Here is a recipe for a salad, shown above, picked fresh from her garden, 90 percent of which consists of wild plants. Susun harvests her "weeds" regularly for culinary and medicinal purposes. Fresh nasturtium leaves have a peppery taste, and Brassica species greens, whether cultivated kale and purple mustard or wild peppergrass, are sharp-flavored. Because this is an unusual salad, the botanical names of the plants are included in the recipe. Serve with a simple dressing made with an herbal vinegar (recipe follows—keep in mind that the herbal vinegar takes 6 weeks to cure) to enhance the "wild" flavors.

Serves 2

2 nasturtium flowers and 8 leaves (Tropaeolum majus)
6 red clover blossoms (Trifolium pratense)
6–8 tender young plantain leaves (Plantago major)
2 stalks lamb's quarter greens and seeds (Chenopodium album)
12 peppergrass leaves (Lepidium sativum)
2 kale leaves (Brassica oleracea acephala)
2 purple mustard leaves (Brassica nigra)
6 catnip leaves (Nepeta cataria)
6 violet leaves (Viola species)
4 dandelion leaves (Taraxacum officinale)

Simple Dressing

Makes 1 pint

2 cups olive oil
1 tablespoon herb vinegar (recipe follows)
1 tablespoon tamari
½ teaspoon garlic powder

Wash and dry the leaves and flowers. Arrange them on a salad plate or in a salad bowl.

To make the dressing: in medium bowl mix olive oil, vinegar, tamari, and garlic powder. (To increase or decrease the recipe, keep in mind that the proportion should be 95 percent oil, 2 percent vinegar, 2 percent tamari, and 1 percent garlic.)

Herb Vinegar

Fill a wide-mouth glass jar full of one fresh herb of your choice. Cover herb with good-quality (preferably apple cider) vinegar at room temperature, filling jar to brim. Cork or cover with a plastic lid. Keep in a cool, dark place for 6 weeks. (Susun Weed points out that if you begin at a new moon, it will be ready by the second full moon.) Remove herbs before using.

CHAPTER THREE

HOUSEHOLD
HERBS
WITH
RECIPES

Scenting the home with herbs is an ancient practice and one of the most rewarding applications of the fragrant herbs. The most ancient peoples on earth used herbs as incense and perfume, and later herbs were employed to scent linen and as strewing agents on the floors of their homes to keep the air fresh and to deter disease. It is merely for convenience that most of us use the prepackaged products available today for scent. But once you have breathed in the marvelous fragrances of household herbs for scent or slept on a pillow made from herbs, the substitutes simply won't do.

Household herbs can also be used for a number of practical purposes, many of which have been replaced by gadgetry. For example, the herb teasel was once used to tease the nap on wool to make it fluffier, and there is no reason why it shouldn't be employed for that purpose today. Many household herbs, such as roses and lavender, have been used to create a sweet-scented furniture polish, while a bunch of horsetails (Equisetum arvense) was considered the perfect agent with which to do the polishing. In the past, people created all fabric colors from natural dyes. This is a complicated process and takes some forbearance to master, but if it is of particular interest, you should consider seeking out sources for how to create brilliant and earthy colors with such herbs as pokeroot, indigo, woad, and madder.

Most of the household herbs within this chapter have a very sweet fragrance, and their mere presence in the home in floral bouquets may be all you wish to do to scent the home with them. Others have insect-repellent qualities and are best used in potpourri-type mixtures that can be placed among linen and clothing. Still others you may wish to dry whole to appreciate simply for their beauty; most retain their ambrosial scents even when dried as everlastings. Herbs are the most versatile of all plants, and many of these household herbs will also have other applications. As you plan your herb garden, try to select herbs that will serve multiple purposes, some as ancient as the dawn of civilization.

The underground stems of many European irises, below, are powdered to produce orris, whose violet scent is used in perfumes and potpourri. Also a classic ingredient for perfumery, cistus, opposite, is a cherished Old World shrub with wrinkled-linen petals that release a lemony fragrance after an early summer rainfall.

Artemisia vulgaris
MUGWORT, CRONEWORT

The ancient Eurasian herb mugwort looks every bit its age. This feathery plant with toothed leaves, purple stems, and flowering spikes has a stylized, antique air about it. So elegant in form, mugwort subtly decorates European and North American meadows in autumn with its delicate yellow flowers.

In the past, plants with noteworthy perfumes were revered because it was thought that they had a special power to fight witches and dispel demons. Whether this smell was lovely or foul, it was still thought to hold some special power; many were worshiped, a practice that was thought to incur a kind of grudging respect among members of the dark forces—and therefore the plants became useful in keeping evil beings in line. Mugwort, with its delicious, aromatic, sagelike smell, naturally became a revered plant in Europe and Asia.

In Europe it was long considered one of the most powerful plants of the field. In England and France garlands involving mugwort and other powerful natural objects—white lilies, birch, fennel, Saint John's wort, and even bird's claws—were once made. These unusual concoctions, which would have been right at home in the naturalistic Dutch school of flower arranging, were thought to have fabulous supernatural powers and probably frightened many a small child into a lifetime of belief in this custom.

A modern-day "green witch"—an herbalist who works closely with plants on a healing and folkloric level—believes that the plant should be called cronewort, a more evocative name, referring to its witchly associations rather than to its old usage in beer-making (hence the word *mug*). It grows uncultivated outside her front door, which recalls the old continental custom of planting mugwort outside the front door of the village herbalist.

Being such a powerful herb, mugwort has long been thought to have the power to predict the future. If you want to determine the course of a relationship and don't want to pay a psychic or fuss with tarot cards, test this old-fashioned technique: Plant two mugworts side by side in well-drained soil in full sun. Designate one as you and the other as your intended. You won't have to wait long for results; mugwort grows easily from seed. If the plants grow toward one another, everything will be wonderful in the relationship. If they bend in opposite directions, problems will inevitably arise (staking is not allowed).

So as not to make self-fulfilling prophecies and create a sense of doom in an otherwise happy relationship, it's best to apply this technique to the lives of your friends and then boldly make detailed predictions about *them* based on the results. Create a whole row of divining mugworts, and don't limit their predictions to love—expand your focus to foretell the course of a business deal, predict whether a nephew will stay in medical school, and augur the possibility of a year-end bonus—anything that can be predicted positively or negatively by the plants growing together or apart. The law of averages states that you will be right at least half the time, and in the meantime you will have amazed your friends with your herbal prowess while also rewarding yourself with a healthy crop of mugwort plants.

Mugworts are good for more than divination. They are wonderful, magically scented household herbs. Dry them and use the leaves for fragrant sleep pillows. Folk belief has it that they will give you pleasant, Technicolor-crisp dreams.

Once dried, mugwort strikes out on a second life. Combined with other herbs, it can be used in potpourri and dream pillow mixtures, above, or in lovely autumnal door swags, opposite left. During the drying process, it will infuse the home with a magical scent, opposite right.

Dream Pillow Mixture

Some herbs have natural soporific qualities and have been used for centuries to induce relaxation. This dream pillow mixture, crafted by Anne Salomon of Tweefontein Herb Farm in New York State, draws on classic sleep-inducing herbs. Its delicate scent is supposed to bring pleasant dreams. If you wish to make a smaller or larger pillow than this one, adjust the amounts so that the hops are one-quarter the amount of the other ingredients, which are used in equal amounts. This is because hops are very light and bulky and also because the somewhat bitter smell can be off-putting to some noses.

Makes 1 6¼-ounce pillow

1 ounce mugwort
1 ounce lemon verbena
1 ounce chamomile flowers
1 ounce pink rosebuds
1 ounce peppermint
¼ ounce hops

All materials should be dried before use. After they are mixed together, either place them in a bowl beside your night table or sew them into a muslin bag and place it within your pillowcase.

Hedeoma pulegioides
AMERICAN PENNYROYAL
Mentha pulegium
EUROPEAN PENNYROYAL

The first settlers of the New World probably arrived pennyroyalless from having exhausted their supplies of the herb while at sea. At that time it was a popular seasickness remedy of sailors and was recommended by the old herbalists as a means of keeping drinking water fresh. Soon after the colonists dragged their sea-weary bodies to shore, they struck out on expeditions to see what plants could replace beloved European favorites.

Some of them might have really longed for a cup of organ-tea, as the beverage made from European pennyroyal was known, to stave off a cold. Others might have craved some pudding-grass—a colloquial name for pennyroyal—to make a batch of classic English "haggas-pudding." Probably everyone sought out the venerable herb to fight off the whole new repertoire of insects they had to deal with in the North American wild, as pennyroyal has insect-repellent qualities.

The colonists must have been quite dismayed not to find European pennyroyal in the New World. It was such a household staple that their quality of life would certainly suffer without it. But upon closer inspection, the colonists' efforts were rewarded. In fields and open woodlands they came upon the delicate, tiny purple flowers of a plant that greatly resembled their old friend. Even in aroma, this delightful doppelgänger was similar, exuding a marvelous, appealing scent, which prompted them to briskly set to work harvesting it for the same wonderful household usages as for European pennyroyal—for use in healing teas and for repelling all manner of flies, fleas, gnats, ticks, and other winged visitors to the home. The plant they found, *Hedeoma pulegioides,* came to be known as American pennyroyal. Both it and European pennyroyal are members of the marvelous mint family.

The two plants' applications in their native lands were remarkably similiar. Native Americans had been using the North American plant externally for centuries to treat skin irritations and keep bugs away and in tea to cure headaches. In Europe, pennyroyal had been known since at least the Roman statesman Pliny the Elder's time, employed to deter fleas—hence its specific name, derived from *pulex,* or flea. It was also used frequently in medicinal teas to cure sundry problems.

Nowadays pennyroyal is no longer widely considered a safe medicinal plant, even in tea, but its marvelous repellent properties are still cherished in the home. To put either pennyroyal to use, consider handcrafting a sachet of dried pennyroyal to scent your wardrobe and linens while also curbing interest from the insect world in your best wool sweater.

Growing both American and European pennyroyal is always a possibility, but it's also a game of mixing and matching your garden's conditions with the herb you prefer. If your soil is naturally dry, *Hedeoma* will take to it; if it's moist, traditional pennyroyal will feel more at home. Pennyroyal has a low, flat growth habit and pretty, elliptical leaves; to most eyes it is prettier than the weedier-looking American variety, which grows higher and has thinner leaves. But, in the same way a French Empire settee looks like a monstrosity in a room decorated with American crafts, everything depends on context. The New World plant would surely outshine European pennyroyal in a meadow

Weedy rambling American pennyroyal grows modestly in an East Coast garden, above left. Its more vain European cousin displays lovely leaves Rapunzel style, right.

of native North American wildflowers. The European variety would give a far more picturesque effect sheathing a hillside in delicate green sprigs or growing on the bank of a stream, near the moisture it so loves. So assess your needs and keep in mind that, despite their looks, both plants are equally useful in the household.

Pennyroyal and Lavender Potpourri

The old-fashioned practice of making potpourri requires so little time but brings such marvelous results. Keep in mind that scents may dissipate quickly if a few simple steps are not taken to ensure freshness. Usually scents are held in the potpourri through fixatives. This unusual herbal blend, shown opposite below, was developed by Connie Wolfe of New York City and has particularly long-lasting qualities because it incorporates cedar shavings, which eliminate the need for a fixative. She advises that if the scent begins to wane, you can "pinch" the pennyroyal and lavender to perk it up. Use air-dried lavender and pennyroyal for this potpourri; either American or European pennyroyal will do.

Makes 3 ounces

1 ounce cedar shavings
1¾ ounces French lavender
¼ ounce pennyroyal

Mix the ingredients and place in a traditional potpourri bowl so the mixture can exude its spicy, woodsy scent. Since both lavender and pennyroyal have strong insect-repellent qualities, it's also a nice idea to sew up the mixture into a pillow and put it in a dresser drawer or put it in a cloth drawstring bag and hang it in the closet to repel moths.

Hesperis matronalis
SWEET ROCKET

Most flowers hoard all their glory for daytime, when many of us are too busy with the trappings of quotidian life to really appreciate their charms. Sweet rocket runs on a more humane, unhurried schedule, looking beautiful and demurely releasing hints of its scent during the day but reserving the fullness of its ethereal perfume for nightfall—just when busy souls can manage to take a daily constitutional in the garden or simply unwind in a cushioned lawn chair. The plant is native to Italy and environs, and the relaxed pace at which it gets around to exuding its perfume is totally in keeping with a southern European temperament.

Sweet rocket's botanical name derives from a Greek word meaning "vesper," or "evening." As an old folk saying goes, at night sweet rocket will "let the delicious secret out / To every breeze that roams about." But sweet rocket also has much to recommend it during the day, owing to its good looks. It is an antique garden flower, mentioned by Pliny the Elder in his writings in the first century A.D. It later became a great favorite in the humble garden plots of European cottagers, who planted these tall, branching night owls in cheerful groups.

There are both single- and double-flowered types that are snowy white or delicately tinged rose, purple, or mauve. Because of its pastel coloration, the plant came to be associated with femininity, earning the name *Violettes des Dames* in France (not to mention the womanly species name *matronalis*). The white sweet rocket was a favorite of Marie-Antoinette, who had it brought to her in prison.

Sweet rocket has been grown in the herb garden for varying purposes across the centuries. It has a history as a medicinal herb, as the dried leaves were once used to treat scurvy. It has often been confused with another plant named salad rocket (arugula), *Eruca sativa*. Both rockets have lance-shaped leaves and four-petaled flowers that bloom in late spring or early summer. Salad rocket, as its name implies, is used as a salad herb, and its leaves have a peppery, spicy taste. Sweet rocket's leaves have also been used for this purpose, but they are very bitter and not worth harvesting. This pretty plant is best used as a household herb to scent potpourris and sachets.

This charming, feminine plant can be grown from seed in the garden and favors a sunny location. It is happy in the herb garden, but if you especially adore its lovely scent, plant a group of sweet rocket under your bedroom window—its seductive fragrance will waft up at night and give you charmed sleep.

The French queen had a reputation for extravagance and craftiness and may have been especially attracted to sweet rocket for its folkloric associations. European lore had it that because the flower does not reveal its fragrance until night, it is a fitting emblem for deceit. Other unkind remarks have been made about sweet rocket. Some garden writers have accused the plant of being rangy and lacking in grace because of its branching habit, but they had probably never seen several sweet rocket plants massed together in the garden on a summer day, their pert petals suspended like colored snowflakes or tiny whirligigs. And they probably were also morning people up with the lark but fading by sunset, never around for sweet rocket's nocturnal scented display.

Sweet rocket conjures up fresh, sweet thoughts of a country childhood. Here it grows with other scented flowers: Guernsey stock and the roses 'Duchesse de Montabele' and 'Charles Austin'.

Hyssopus officinalis
HYSSOP

When romantic country customs were still actively observed in England, roughly up to Victorian times, the first balmy breezes of May signaled that the feast of Whitsun was coming. Although it was a church event, there was no dread of long, stuffy church services, no fear of interminable lectures on the wickedness of temporal pleasures, for Whitsun—sometimes also known as Whit Sunday—was a day of merriment and festivities, a celebration of everything wonderful, sweet, and cheerful about spring.

On the day of this feast, which fell fifty days after Easter and today is represented by Pentecost, revelers would put on their most flirtatious clothes (fresh linen shirts for men, fine white embroidery decorating sheer muslin for women) and follow the merrily clanging bells to the church, which would be suffused with sweet smells and lovely, fragrant spring flowers and foliage. Among those plants decorating the church would be hyssop, on account of its pleasant aroma. After the service the countryfolk might attend a Whitsun Ale, held by the church, at which they would consume ale with fervor. After drinking a substantial amount, they would be entreated by angelic-looking parish girls to make a contribution to the church. Of course, the revelers would generously comply in good cheer.

Bolstered by the heady beverage, the Whitsun celebrants might decide to pay a visit to the churchyard. Everyone was expected to partake of the May merriment, even if only in spirit. Friends and relatives of the deceased would take along armfuls of pleasant-scented plants to strew on the graves, and hyssop, chamomile, rosemary, sweet-williams, mignonette, and thyme were the essentials. Not only would this create a festive air in the graveyard, but it also deterred any evil beings from residing there: plants with strong smells had long been thought to have power against evil.

After all this activity, it would be time to hurry home for Whitsun dinner. Traditionally duckling was served, and as was popular in bygone days, it would be garnished with hyssop. British countryfolk celebrating the charming customs of Whitsun probably hardly even noticed the presence of hyssop, as it was such a standard part of their lives. Hyssop had been known in Britain and on the Continent since at least the tenth century, when Benedictine monks flavored their liqueurs with it. Its name is thought to derive from a Hebrew word meaning "holy herb," indicating an antique usage as a cleansing herb. The British cottagers' homes were also filled with the plant, as it was a strewing herb used to deter pests and keep household residents healthy with its minty, oddly medicinal odor, a practice transported to America with the Puritans.

When the plant came into flower, they would gather the coquettish blue or violet flowers and add them to scented nosegays filled with other herbs with sweet-smelling or antiseptic qualities, such as rosemary, thyme, southernwood, and roses. These were especially popular in times of the plague, for they not only masked the odors of the streets but were thought to protect their carriers from disease. The endlessly romantic Victorians assigned individual plants special meaning and thus constructed nosegays with deeply encoded messages, which ranged from lyrical floral love notes to symbolic poison pen letters. Hyssop's assigned meaning was "cleanliness," a reference to its camphorlike odor, and in a nosegay it was the equivalent of declaring one's intentions to be pure.

Whether it truly has antiseptic qualities is debatable, but many scientists concur that the volatile oils of hyssop might have the

power to kill germs. Certainly its use as a household herb is still viable, for its minty odor in potpourris and sachets is preferable to manufactured bottled scents.

Hyssop was used in medieval times as a potherb to mask the taste of less than prime meats, but today you may wish to limit culinary uses to the fresh leaves brewed in an aromatic tea or, recalling the Whitsun tradition, as a garnish for duck, used sparingly.

It is not an herb you are likely to see growing in the average herb garden, but why not revive the tradition in your own? Plants can still be had today. Growing hyssop adds a rarefied, ancient air to the herb garden, and its antique scent will inspire you to dream of old customs and merry processions through a churchyard.

Here grows hyssop in a Swedish convent herb garden—near the tombstone of a nun who died in 1795, left. Perhaps the nuns who lived here grew hyssop in reference to a verse from the Bible: "Purge me with hyssop, and I shall be clean; wash me, and I shall be whiter than snow." Or maybe they followed the example of Benedictine monks of the Middle Ages, who used the herb as a flavoring in their liqueurs.

Lavandula angustifolia ENGLISH LAVENDER
Lavandula stoechas FRENCH LAVENDER

It is a mistake to assume that everyone who gardens likes nothing better than to spend all leisure hours burrowing about on hands and knees and fussing with "difficult" plants. Certainly there are the Weeders, Pruners, and Compulsive Collectors and Planters (everyone seems to have a very worried-looking uncle who fits this profile), but there is also a lesser-known but thriving breed called the Passives or Laissez-Faires. Those people who disdainfully pronounce the latter name "lazy" are quite mistaken. There's certainly nothing wrong with the idea of passive gardening—of putting great effort into getting a garden going but then sitting back and watching it take form, with minimal interference in the form of watering and such. This is Type B gardening, and it suits many people just fine.

It also sits well with lavender, the most glorious scented herb of all, used and loved for centuries for its aromatic qualities. But lavender also gives the Pruners and Compulsive Collectors much to think about and act on. This pleasantly scented plant easily adjusts to as little or as much care as you decide to lavish on it. And there are lovely forms to choose from and collect, including rich purple types and a rare white variety, *L. angustifolia* 'Alba', which can be planted in ghostly drifts in the garden.

This irresistible herb is easy to grow and will even put up with drought conditions; in general it enjoys well-drained soil, a habit that harks back to its Mediterranean origins. Once established from cuttings, it doesn't require a great deal of upkeep. Hardy varieties of English lavender such as 'Hidcote' and 'Munstead'— named for the home of Gertrude Jekyll, who developed it—weather cold winters fairly well, especially when protected by a warm blanket of pine boughs. The tender types, which can be grown year-round outdoors in frost-free climates, can be brought into the greenhouse or grown as potted windowsill plants in northern climes.

The extent to which you prune lavender is your choice. Some gardeners constantly trim off dead flowers and keep the foliage in line. Others prefer just to let these remain on the plant to weather: like seedpods, the grayish foliage and faded purple heads have their own regal charm. As a middle ground, prune lavender in early spring to strengthen the plant. Harvest the flower heads as the buds begin to open; then air-dry them.

Lavender even accommodates a range of garden aesthetics. The sighing romantic comfortably entrenched in a rambling Victorian manse, and desirous of making a garden in the nineteenth-century manner, is well advised to choose lavender for the design—keeping in mind that it can quickly come to the rescue in case of a dramatic faint, as it was a classic Victorian swooning herb. Victorian gardens took on many quirky forms and were often patterned to look like carpets or even resemble naturalistic forms, such as bird's feet. Lavender could easily be incorporated into such styles, perhaps alternating with the gray-green foliage of rosemary or the bluish foliage of rue.

The more reserved, brass-tacks gardener would probably opt to grow lavender in the herbaceous border or as an edging plant along a walkway. In seventeenth-century

French lavender L. stoechas var. pedunculata is so sensuous looking, above, it is no wonder that it is used as a massage oil. Danish floral artist Tage Anderson creates topiaries made from spikes of English and Spanish lavender, opposite.

Ireland lavender was used as a fragrant lawn plant and was trimmed low. For the gardener who simply can't choose between styles, lavenders are a soft and subtle intermediary plant between the landscaped grounds surrounding a home and the wild woodland garden. Planting lavender in undulating drifts makes for enchanting results, reminiscent of the vast fields of lavender in the south of France.

Lavender also has the ability to fine-tune color in the garden. It profoundly affects everything planted around it with its muted foliage tones, creating an intense tapestry effect when plants with dark green leaves are planted nearby—each seeming to be more intensely colored as a result of the interplay. The flowers, too, have pretty tones that range from light violet to rich, royal purple. Lavender in the gray garden creates a patina, like that of a fine old carpet whose colors, though subtle, have depth. Try combining lavender with the gray-tinged foliage of the herbs southernwood *(Artemisia abrotanum)*, mugwort *(Artemisia vulgaris)*, lamb's ears *(Stachys byzantina)*, and rue *(Ruta graveolens)*.

Lavender's gardenesque qualities offer so much enticement that it is difficult to believe that lavender was first grown not as an ornamental plant at all—it wasn't considered particularly beautiful by ancient gardeners, and until the eighteenth century, garden writers considered it almost homely, but certainly serviceable. Lavender's use as a scenting agent for washing water extends back to the time of the ancient Greeks and Romans (the genus name derives from the Latin *lavare*, "to wash"). It is believed that French lavender *(L. stoechas)* was the species used.

French lavender has stunning velvety deep purple bracts that seem to extend as if in prayer above the flower. It is traditionally associated with medicinal usages, although the applications of all the lavenders are the same. A diluted oil can be used for cleaning wounds, on bites and stings, and as an aid to massage. It is said that sniffing the oil or

rubbing the diluted oil or lavender water on the temples can ease headaches; in the time of the great British herbal writers lavender was widely recommended as a cure for melancholy.

English lavender—with gorgeous dark purple, pink, and bluish flowers—is a classic household herb and is the type of lavender used for centuries in Britain as an insect repellent. It is traditionally placed in hospital sickrooms as a fumigant because of its natural disinfectant and insect-repellent qualities as well as its uplifting fragrance. It was probably English lavender that the seventeenth-century fishing writer Isaak Walton (author of *The Compleat Angler, or the Contemplative Man's Recreation,* whose subject matter seems strangely contemporary and fashionable) was thinking of when he wrote: "I long to be in a house where the sheets smell of lavender." This is a reference to the age-old practice of placing sweet lavender spikes among linens to scent and protect them from insects. Walton was understandably enchanted by lavender's soothing aroma, and more than likely he coveted the smell so much because he hoped to mask the odors of his pastime. Another old usage of lavender is to light the spikes and let them smolder like incense to scent a room. Of course, there are other aromatic applications for lavender, the most well known being potpourris and sachets.

There is much about lavender to please. Even cooks find uses for the plant, using the small flower buds in minute quantities as an herbal spice. The flower arranger might want to place the spikes in a topiary or lovely scented wreath. And the Passive Gardener will take simple delight in breathing in the delicious aroma while daydreaming in the hammock.

At Capel Manor in England, lavender 'Hidcote Blue' grows among poppies, roses, foxglove, and peach-bells, left. The lavender might be harvested for potpourri or for a soothing herbal bath mixed with rosemary, mint, and comfrey.

Medicago scutellata
SNAKES, SNAILS, AND HEDGEHOGS
MEDICK CLOVER
Trifolium repens
COMMON CLOVER

When a young surgeon named William Roxburgh left Scotland for India in 1776, appointed by his government to act as an assistant surgeon, he found it difficult to leave his small home garden behind. To make him feel more at home in the foreign land, he planted a small herb garden filled with the economic and medicinal plants he had come to depend on at home. In those days, being in the medical field meant that one was intimately familiar with the habits of plants.

Relying on his garden for comfort and sustenance, Roxburgh toughed it out remarkably well for quite a few years. Along the way he also took an interest in native Indian plants and sent home many a beautiful botanical drawing done by local artists for the appreciation of those back home. Amid all the exotic plants of India, though, until he resigned in 1813, he continued to tend a patch of humble English plants, many considered weeds at home, in his garden. Among his dandelions, hemlock, plantain, and sorrel was clover, *Trifolium repens.*

The humble white and red clovers of Europe, now common sights in meadows in North America, have been taken for granted for centuries. Yet these inconspicuous-looking *Trifolium* genus plants have been used for herbal remedies for centuries. The common white clover has a long history in European folk medicine. A healing tea was once made from its flowers, and a salve made from the small pretty blossoms was also once used to soothe wounds.

There were also culinary usages, although the plant could never hope to win a place among the *fines herbes*: the dried flowers and seed heads were used to make bread during Irish famines, and some Americans have used the leaves as a salad herb. *T. pratense* has been used as a dye plant for its lovely red color, and a delicately flavored tea was brewed by the herbally knowledgeable for medicinal purposes. It's best to think of the *Trifolium* clovers' culinary usages more as historical curiosities than anything else.

Their lovely foliage also creates an antique touch in the herb patch. The leaves will occasionally (and arbitrarily) grow in groups of four rather than three, resulting in the symbol-laden four-leaf clover—the significance of which is obvious even to those who haven't studied botanical folklore. The normal three-leaf pattern resulted in the plant being associated in ancient religions with triad goddesses. Christianity updated the tradition to designate the plant as representative of the Christian Trinity, and the Irish have periodically claimed it as the shamrock, the sacred plant of Saint Patrick. The appearance of a fourth leaf was thought to signify Christ's cross. And so four-leaf clovers were plucked whenever found because they were thought to help cure diseases, stave off evil, and generally fulfill the wildest fantasies imaginable. The queen's clover, *T. repens* 'Atropurpureum,' is especially efficient at producing four leaves.

Another plant that lays strong claim to being the true four-leaf clover belongs to a different genus entirely. *Medicago lupulina,* black nonesuch, is regarded by purist Irish as the true shamrock. Clover is a curious catchall name for some of the plants that are members of the pea family.

The medick clovers have a most curious history. Like the four-leaf clover of their sister *Trifolium* genus, the medick clovers boast a few of their own structural anomalies. These plants were once grown in the garden as something akin to sideshow freaks. Along with several other bizarre-looking plant genera, they were grouped under the name "Caterpillars; Snakes, Snails, and Hedgehogs; Worms; Horns; Half-moons; and Horseshoes"—a description that would arouse any gardener's interest.

All these plants strongly resembled what their common name described and were a great garden hit from the seventeenth to the nineteenth centuries in Europe and also in the households of American gardeners who felt it was worth the trouble to order them from overseas. In typical, extreme Victorian-era fashion, hosts hid the leguminous fruits of those plants known as caterpillars, worms, and snakes, snails, and hedgehogs under lettuce leaves in salads or floated them in soups to surprise their guests in the same manner as the contemporary canned snake. It's not known if they were actually eaten, so again you must take these as symbolic culinary herbs.

Perhaps the most beautiful-looking medick clover is *Medicago sculetta,* known commonly as "Snakes, Snails, and Hedgehogs." John Parkinson described this plant as "The plant that beareth these pretty toyes for Gentlewomen." Its spirally coiled fruits do resemble those of a snail. It would be difficult to obtain these herbs of yesteryear for your garden, but there is a renewed interest in such odd plants—if you scan the listings of nurseries with unusual plants, you may just get lucky. If you should locate them, they grow best on sunny slopes in neutral soil, out of the way of foot traffic and curious children who might try to harvest them as pets.

Snakes, snails, and hedgehogs graces the garden at Hatfield House, opposite above left. Queen's clover, opposite above right, is apt to be four-leaved. Wearing it might enable you to see fairies. Common clover and bistort combine in a simple arrangement, opposite below.

Monarda didyma
BEE BALM, BERGAMOT

The blaring red color of traditional forms of bee balm is the first signal that this is a plant inspiring excitement, even revolution. During the high-spirited aftermath of the famous Boston Tea Party of 1773, when the American colonists drank anything but traditional black tea to protest the home country's tax, bee balm tea was the beverage of choice. It was known then as Oswego Tea, a reference to the name of the county in New York State named for the tribe of Native Americans that lived there and enjoyed bee balm tea themselves. (As was the case with most useful North American flora, the colonists purloined customs from the Native American and claimed them as their own.) The colonists found its lively citrusy taste reason enough to drink it. But the colonists took the Indian custom a step further and introduced it as an ornamental plant in their dooryard gardens. Also, they grew the flowers to dry for lovely home decoration arrangements and for potpourri.

Bee balm's outcoiled blossoms resemble a beautiful spider. The American botanist John Bartram, who frequently traded plants with European growers, quickly recognized the outstanding beauty of the plant and shipped it off to the English grower Peter Collinson in 1744, soon after coming across it on one of his plant-seeking journeys into New York and Canada. In those days governments did not strictly control plant importation, and species were merrily traded back and forth without impoundment by customs. Soon after the first seeds of bee balm arrived in England, the plant was being sold at Covent Garden in London.

It wasn't the first plant of the *Monarda* genus to embark from its native land. In 1637 the plant hunter John Tradescant the Younger squirreled away seeds of the pink- or lilac-colored wild bergamot *(M. fistulosa)* that he brought back with him from Virginia to England. There it became known as an oregano *(Oreganum fistulosum)* and was dubbed a "wild mint of America."

In fact the *Monardas* are members of the mint family that grow in fragrant pockets across the North American continent, usually under the name horsemint, presumably because of their coarse, unruly appearance, which resembles a horse's spreading tail. Bee balm, the most beautiful and cultured of this checkered lot, received its common name bergamot because of the resemblance to the smell of the bergamot orange tree. The plant also has quite a few other names, depending on whom you're talking to. In the northeastern United States it might be called blue balm, high balm, low balm, mountain balm, or mountain mint. In Appalachia, where the residents float the flowers in iced tea and lemonade, the plant is known as red bee balm and red horsemint.

There is a myth in Dorset, England, that sprang up around the plant soon after it was introduced, claiming that it will heap nothing but sickness and calamity on whoever brings the plant indoors. But there are many people living happy lives with bee balm right in the pantry, so this antiquated belief should not deter you from harvesting the leaves and flowers for your own culinary purposes. Make an edible centerpiece using the flowers from which guests can pluck fresh petals to garnish food. Imitate the Appalachians and toss the flowers in punch or add them to cool summer beverages for flavor and a jolt of scarlet color. Or dry the leaves to make the famous patriotic tea.

This is not a plant suited to a garden of muted pastels or one that relies on subtle interrelations among plant forms. Grow bee balm if you want to give your garden some vertical definition and a splash of color. Its frilly form, three-foot stature, and pronounced coloration make it an imposing addition to the garden. In her remarkable book *Flowers and Their Histories*, the always frank Alice M. Coats summons up genuine enthusiasm for this North American native and does not resent the plant in the slightest for its role in rebelling against her motherland: "Few plants so successfully contrive to have the best of both worlds," she pens, "combining fragrant leaves with brilliant flowers; indeed, its only rivals in this respect are some of the hybrid sweet-briars." Do not plant bee balm in the same bed with your traditional culinary herbs; it prefers a moist, fertile soil. You may be tempted to plant hybrid forms, which come in a range of colors, but remember that the red type will especially catch the eye of hummingbirds, who love to feast on its nectar.

Garden Party Centerpiece

This herbal centerpiece, created by Pat Reppert and Vonnie Bragg of Shale Hill Farm in upstate New York, combines a number of beautiful herbs and is lovely for a garden party. A variation on this might include not household and edible herbs as used here, but edible herbs alone. The plants for this centerpiece, shown opposite page, were plucked in summer. Afterwards it was brought indoors, where it scented the home for days. The plants are placed in Oasis foam, which keeps flowers fresh. This centerpiece can be adapted to different seasons. For example, in spring, elder blossoms mixed with foliage in gray and green shades are spectacular, complemented by a vivid red strawberry Maywine punch. In autumn you might incorporate such herbs as goldenrod, dried globe amaranth, sweet annie, and staghorn sumac. In winter, juniper and ivy make a nice mix.

wire wreath base
punch bowl, glass tray, or pizza pan
Oasis foam
30 to 40 sprigs boxwood (Buxus
    sempervirens)
30 to 40 sprigs juniper (Juniperus 'Blue
    Ray')
15 to 20 sprigs artemisia (Artemisia
    Purshiana)
6 to 8 sprigs lamb's ears (Stachys
    byzantina)
6 to 8 sprigs feverfew (Chrysanthemum
    Parthenium)
6 to 8 sprigs silver speedwell (Veronica
    officinalis)
6 to 8 yarrow flowers (Achillea millefolium)
6 to 8 bee balm flowers (Monarda didyma)

6 to 8 lily flowers (Lilium orientale
    'Stargazer')
6 to 10 ivy leaves (Hedera helix)

Select a wire base large enough to fit
around the base of your punch bowl but
small enough to fit inside a glass tray. Cut
Oasis foam to fit in a wire wreath base,
wedging the foam into the base. Secure it in
place with floral wire. Place plants in the
foam, beginning with box and juniper,
which provide a lovely, aromatic evergreen
base. Follow with grays and whites:
artemisia, lamb's ears, feverfew flowers,
and silver speedwell. End with the eye-
catching, focal flowers: yellow yarrow,
bright red bee balm, and lily. Prevent

withering of the blooms by hardening them
off. This involves cutting the stems on a
diagonal and placing them in warm water
for 24 hours. You might also ensure long
life for the lilies by inserting their stems in
individual florist's water picks and
inserting these into the foam. Add ivy
leaves to camouflage the water picks if you
wish. If you don't use water picks, it should
be easy enough simply to insert the stems
into the foam, but if you have trouble,
reinforce the stems with florist's picks and
cover the joins with green floral tape. Add
punch bowl to the center of the wreath, on
top of tray.

Papaver orientale
ORIENTAL POPPY
Papaver rhoeas
CORN POPPY
FIELD POPPY
FLANDERS POPPY
Papaver somniferum
OPIUM POPPY

Almost two hundred years ago in England, at the height of the Industrial Revolution, poor working-class women in Manchester and other urban factory centers sought solace from their workaday woes at teatime. They would brew up a cheap beverage, affectionately known as "loddy," which gave them a brief, dreamy respite from the factory life. It consisted of opium—a substance produced from *Papaver somniferum,* which was grown widely on a commercial scale in England—mixed with wine. The beverage was consumed avidly. Factory production must have hit a near-standstill in the late afternoons, similar to the aftereffects of the liquid lunch today.

People in the twenty-first century will probably react to tobacco usage in this century with the same horror with which we now regard the casual use of opium in the nineteenth and previous centuries. The brilliant English poet Samuel Taylor Coleridge is one famous casualty of the drug; although opium helped inspire the

Field poppies spring up naturally in this cottage garden, right. The opium poppy, opposite, opens in a flourish on a warm summer day.

fantastical "Kubla Khan," it eventually was his undoing. As a result of these narcotic associations, the poppy has a lurid image for some. The famous scene in *The Wizard of Oz* in which the wicked witch dopes poor Dorothy and her cohorts with a field of poppies has not done much for this plant's reputation. It is especially shocking to learn that the American Shakers concocted an opium-based syrup to give to high-strung children at bedtime.

But we should not simply look askance at this gorgeous, ancient plant. *P. somniferum* has flowers that can be white, pink, red, or purple, and an elegant pedigree to match. Unfortunately for American gardeners its cultivation is controlled by special license, but this shouldn't deter any flower lover from learning its heady history. When Napoleon assigned Charles Percier and Pierre Fontaine the task of inventing a new national style, they brushed up on their knowledge of classical motifs and discovered that the poppy was a perfect symbol of classicism. In their decorative motifs of the Empire period, they relied heavily on the poppy's flower and seedpods. Because in

Opium poppy pods make decorative, sculptural elements in indoor arrangements, above and opposite. The pods' contents yield a juice used in medicine for centuries, right.

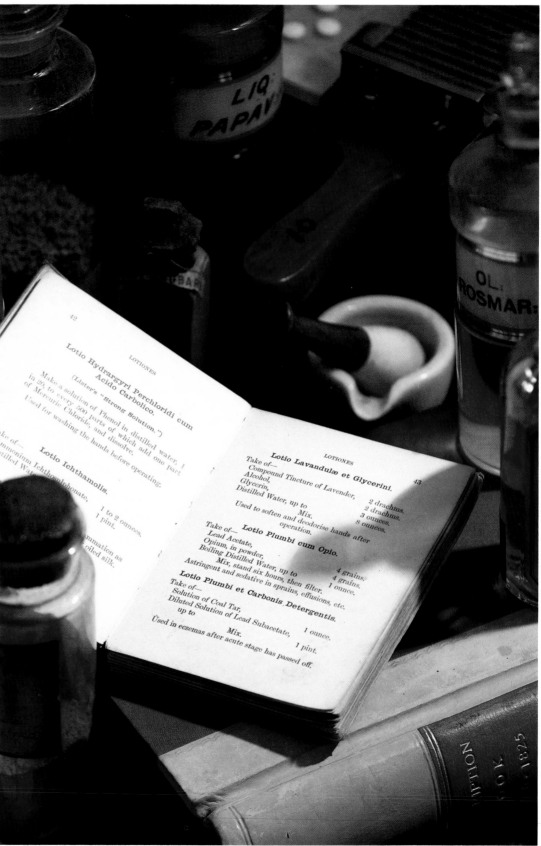

classical times the poppy was the symbol of Hypnos, the Greek god of sleep, and of Morpheus, the Roman god of dreams and night, they used the flower motif especially in bedrooms.

Despite the unfortunate addictive effects of opium use, it is a fascinating plant because of its long history. Opium use began with the ancient Sumerians and was passed on to the Egyptians and Greeks. It was soon taken up in the Middle East. (The poppy is a favored flower there to this day. Once opium has been extracted from the pods, rattling bunches of seedpods are sold in the streets; these are cracked open to yield the completely nonnarcotic seeds for casual eating as one strolls along.) It became a great favorite in Asia, too. The French author and filmmaker Jean Cocteau visited one such establishment in the 1920s and remarked, "Opium is the only vegetable substance that communicates the vegetable state to us."

The famous *Wizard of Oz* scene is actually fallacious, as crude opium is the hardened milky sap of the unripe capsule and is obtained only by a tedious process of cutting the capsule open—it certainly isn't airborne. In India, where growing the opium poppy was especially big commerce in the nineteenth century, a special agricultural implement called the *nashtar* was developed for this purpose, as John Scott explained in his *Manual of Opium Husbandry* of 1877. In nineteenth-century India special trains filled with mango-wood chests of opium made frequent journeys back and forth between the poppy-strewn Ganges plain and Calcutta.

The opium poppy grows today in ornamental European gardens, but not in America. This does not mean that Americans can't put this wonderful plant to use,

In her Victorian-era book An Island Garden, *Celia Thaxter quoted a friend who said of her Oriental poppies, right, "The fire-engines always turn out when my Orientals blaze up on the hillside." Of Shirley poppies, opposite, Thaxter wrote, "I know of no flower that has so many charming tricks and manners, none with a method of growth more picturesque and fascinating."*

however. The seeds are used in cooking—a use that extends back to the original Olympic athletes—in such foods as delicately-flavored poppy seed cakes and hearty poppy seed bagels. And the seedpods are available for flower arrangements and crafts.

Residents of countries where growing the opium poppy is legal should remember Robert Burns's analogy of seeking pleasure to gathering poppies before they pluck the flowers for arrangements: "You seize the flow'r, its bloom is shed." Lucky opium poppy gardeners should resist the urge to bring poppies indoors and simply admire them in the garden. Then, after the plant has faded, allow the seed heads to dry out naturally on the plant from exposure to wind and sun. These are wonderful, magical-looking touches in flower arrangements. Pick some of the heads when they are just gray-green and allow some to turn completely brown for variety. And do leave some on the plants so that you can admire their beautiful skeletonized forms in winter.

The bright red poppy seems to cry "Wake up!" as forcefully as the serene opium poppy encourages sleep. These wonderful plants, legal everywhere, also have a place in herbalism. *Papaver rhoeas,* the common field poppy of Europe, also goes by the names corn, Shirley (a strain of the species), and Flanders poppy—the latter as a result of John McCrae's poem "In Flanders Fields" in which he makes reference to poppies on a battlefield. It has long been a belief that *P. rhoeas* springs up on battlegrounds to commemorate dead soldiers, and this is why the plant is associated with Memorial Day in some parts of America. There was also a belief among early Christians that the first poppies grew where the blood of Christ had stained them red.

While the opium poppy is the symbol of sleep, the field poppy takes this state one step further as the symbol of death. These flowers grew as weeds in the ancient wheat fields of Greece, and farmers took out their aggression on the poor field poppy—as

wheat is the symbol of life, and it was the nemesis of the weed—by designating it the symbol of death. Today not much has changed. Common names European farmers have bestowed on the plant include "headache" and "redweed." Nevertheless, to the nonfarming visitor from abroad the sight of these poppies growing in the field is quite charming. They have such a relaxed, rambling look about them and are extremely cheerful. These flowers are used to obtain a pigment to color medicine and wine, and those who work with dye plants should experiment with this species. The flowers have also been used medicinally and in healing, soothing baths. Another relative to try growing is the Oriental poppy, *P. orientale.* This beautiful poppy, an ancient resident of Armenia, is usually red but can also take on orange or baby pink coloration. The Turkish have been known to feast on the green seeds, but these are thought much too bitter for most people's palates.

Field poppies bloom readily in Europe, left. Once picked, their flowers are short-lived, so it's best to have some household craft—such as creating a dye—in mind before harvesting them.

Rosa damascena
DAMASK ROSE

More so than any other plant, the rose is infused with deep symbolism surrounding every aspect of human existence—from birth to marriage to death. But the rose is more ancient than even the most primitive human rite. Before anything resembling *Homo sapiens* was around to pluck them, *Rosa* species wafted scent into the humid air of prehistory. The closest relatives of those ancient roses that we have are the species roses, known today as old roses. There are modern types of roses with flashier, longer-lasting blooms, but these upstarts seem to clamor for attention in the garden while the old roses hold court serenely, confidently, and elegantly.

The garden writer and novelist Vita Sackville-West gave as high praise to the old roses as any plant could ever hope to receive: "There is nothing scrimpy or stingy about them. They have a generosity which is as desirable in plants as in people." Old roses have the quiet grace and mellowed perfection of port or antique lace, and if there can be just one old rose for the herb garden, let it be the damask.

When Herodotus, the Greek historian of the fifth century B.C., wrote of a magnificent rose that he spotted in the Gardens of Midas, garden historians concur that he probably had a damask variety in mind. It is generally held that when Virgil refers to a

Ephemeral June-blooming damask roses enchant bees in an island garden, opposite. These roses can be preserved for years if plucked at the right moment. Manhattan craftswoman Connie Wolfe creates "fleurpourris" filled with perfectly preserved roses and other flowers with herbal histories: peonies, pinks, globe amaranth, ranunculus, star anise, and peppergrass, right.

rose that blooms twice in one year in his *Georgics,* he is referring to the splendid *R. damascena* 'Bifera', the autumn damask. The damask rose has been in existence for so long that its geographical origin is debatable, although it is thought to have originated in Asia Minor. By the time of the Crusades it was firmly established in Europe.

Hybrids of the damask rose, *R. damascena,* are grouped under the old-rose heading "Damasks," and they have been famous for centuries for their fragrance and velvety pink petals, although there are also red-blossomed types. The flowers of one lovely cultivar, *Versicolor,* the York-and-Lancaster rose, vary from all white to all pink; some have delicate white ribbons lacing through a pink background. This rose is named for the famed fifteenth-century Wars of the Roses in which the houses of York and Lancaster vied for power, each side symbolized by a rose.

No rose is more apt to represent the rich body of lore surrounding all roses than the damask. It is, as Nicholas Culpeper wrote, a rose "under Venus," a case where astrology meets ancient lore since the rose was the ancient Romans' symbol of the love goddess Venus. A Roman myth states that Cupid—the perpetually naked, cherubic son of the love goddess—gave a rose to Harpocrates, the god of silence, so that his mother's amours would be kept secret. Roses, then, have been linked eternally with silence, as the expression *sub-rosa* illustrates. The Romans also found practical applications for the rose: war, feasts, marriage, and death were all occasions to strew, consume, bathe in, or wear rose petals. They believed that if you wore a rose wreath while indulging at a bacchanalia, you wouldn't become intoxicated; the rose's powerful fragrance, they reasoned, was certainly as potent as wine. The rose later

became Christianized in Europe and was associated chastely with the Virgin Mary, absolved of the sins related to its more venturesome days of Venus. Rosary beads were fashioned from rosehips and petals, and roses became incorporated in stained glass and other designs of the Catholic church.

In *Love's Labour's Lost* Shakespeare wrote: "At Christmas I no more desire a rose / Than wish a snow in May's newfangled mirth; But like of each thing that in season grows." Shakespeare might not have approved of the latest trend in perfumery of his day, attar of roses. Its scent so captures the rose's charms that sniffing it in the dead of winter is a powerful reminder of warmer days. In the sixteenth century Europeans discovered how to distill the essential oil from petals of the damask rose to make this luxurious perfume, which is still made today. The damask's petals have also long been used for potpourri. It's likely that your rose petal jam, too, is made from the damask blooms, since this is a time-honored practice known to Culpeper.

With so many centuries of garden service to recommend it, the damask rose surely deserves serious consideration by the historically minded herb grower. Rose culture is not so difficult as might be imagined, especially that of the species roses, which are hardier than the modern hybrids. They prefer full sun and a good garden soil. Roses thrive on fertilization in the spring and an additional fertilization after they have bloomed in June—"the month of leaves and roses," as a Victorian poet wrote. Removing old wood in spring from a rosebush also increases its vigor.

The damask rose will grow up to eight feet high, so use it either in the center of your herb plot, perhaps surrounded by boxwood, or to define the outer limits of the plot with its flowers. Although, like Shakespeare, you'll surely want to savor the rose's beauty while in season, be sure to gather petals for household crafts so that you can enjoy this flower year-round.

Roses sheathe a wall at a Scottish stone farmhouse, opposite, where resident hounds enjoy olfactory bliss in the herb garden out back.

Damask Rose Petal Jam

Feasting on this ambrosial rose petal jam is the closest you will ever come to eating perfume. The secret to this jam's appeal lies in both its taste and its scent—both could be described as sweet, heavenly, inspired, and sprightly. It is delicious by itself, but you will, of course, want to spread it on your favorite bread or perhaps use it as a filling for tarts and cookies. This recipe comes from the versatile Louise Hyde of Well-Sweep Herb Farm in Port Murray, New Jersey. She advises that you use only unsprayed damask roses, especially because such roses do not have a bitter white end to the petal. If other rose petals are used, be sure to remove the white portion of the petal before using.

Makes jam to fill 16 8-ounce jars

10 pounds sugar
2 pounds rose petals
2 quarts water
½ cup fresh lemon juice
¼ pound powdered pectin

In large porcelain pan, place a layer of sugar, then a layer of rose petals, alternating layers until all the rose petals are used up. Create 3 or 4 layers of each ingredient. Cover pan with lid and allow to sit overnight. This extracts the oils and allows them to settle into the sugar.

The following day, add the water and lemon juice. At this point, if you want the petals to be of a smaller size, add the mixture a bit at a time to a blender and blend.

Stir in pectin and place pan over high heat; bring to a full rolling boil, stirring constantly. After mixture has reached a full rolling boil, cook for 2 minutes. Remove from heat. Continue to stir for 8 to 10 minutes. This will prevent the petals from rising to the surface of the jam jar.

Pour jam into clean, sterilized jars and top with paraffin wax. Seal.

CHAPTER FOUR

MEDICINAL
HERBS
WITH
RECIPES

In contemporary terminology "medicine" is associated more with pills and mysterious synthetic concoctions than with anything fresh, green, and smelling of the Earth. Yet herbal medicine's history predates modern medicine by millennia, and its existence today bears witness to its validity. Once reliant on the Doctrine of Signatures, the belief that the look of a plant suggested its medicinal applications, we have learned how to synthesize chemicals. But medicine to a certain extent has come full circle. Today many of the old applications of plants are being looked at with new interest. Feverfew is looked on as a miracle drug for migraine; digitalis derived from foxglove is used for a heart stimulant and regulator, and sweet annie is being tested as a treatment for malaria.

Many of the medicinal herbs of the past are no longer used in that manner, and today we grow them in the herb garden in symbolic form only. By cultivating them, we create a living link with the past and actually create a theme garden of medical history, a reminder of the science of medicine's constant evolution. Presented in this chapter is a selection of herbs with active and antique medicinal usages and a few simple recipes for using them, not so much to cure illness but to enhance health and to soothe.

There are remarkable universalities in the world of medicinal herbs. Many herbs have the same medicinal usages in different cultures. In Chinese herbalism, medicinal herbs can have any of four energies and five flavors. The energies are hot, warm, cold, and cool; the flavors are hot (in a different sense from the energies), sour, bitter, sweet, and salty. This corresponds loosely to Nicholas Culpeper's chart of the "temperaments" of herbs, which are hot,

Images from the Amuse Amused Muses Musing Museum, a private collection at a New York State herbalist's home, guard the precious contents of the herbal medicine chest, right. An herbal bouquet, punctuated by medicinal foxglove and ranunculus, sits on a sunny window ledge at Linnaeus's Uppsala home, opposite.

dry, cool, and moist. Similarly, in the same way that Culpeper's herbs are governed by planets, which in turn govern parts of the body, Chinese herbalism recognizes associations between the vital organs and the five elements: wood, fire, earth, water, and metal. These correlations among herbs, the body, and the solar system underscore their centuries-old importance on every continent.

In all cultures herbs have been revered as healing and protective agents. One of the most eloquent ways that the power of herbs was ever expressed was in the monologue of the medicine man in the ancient Indian Rig Veda:

> From heaven did the host of herbs,
> Come flying down and say to me,
> If we find him still alive,
> Free from harm this man shall be.

Violets, opposite above left, were once believed to cure French pox. Many healing herbs have cosmetic qualities, opposite below left. Stately foxglove, an ancient medicinal, yields a heart sedative, opposite right. Linnaeus's medicine chest contains eighteenth-century potions and powders, right. Feverfew leaves, below, are purported to ease migraine headaches.

Achillea millefolium
COMMON YARROW
SOLDIER'S WOUNDWORT
THOUSAND-SEAL

Remarkable yarrow is probably right at your fingertips, growing along the roadside or in a field near your home. Yet if you aren't acquainted with this vintage healing plant, yarrow will certainly not go out of its way to make its presence known, preferring to blend in with the soft palette of colors in the wildflower meadow. Yarrow is native to Europe and western Asia but has become naturalized as a weed in North America, Australia, and New Zealand. Masquerading as an insignificant, one-of-many plant, yarrow has relieved itself of the burden of medicinal responsibility placed on it by the Europeans who brought the treasured seed thousands of miles just to ensure they would have it in their gardens in their new countries of residence.

Yarrow seems to say, "Oh, pay me no mind. I'm just a useless weed with nothing to do," as it sways nonchalantly in the breeze in meadows from June through to autumn. Throughout its long history yarrow has made many escapes from the garden to attempt to live humbly and anonymously as a weed. In America it has become an itinerant with no permanent garden address—quite literally a hobo taking up residence in the waste areas around railroad tracks. Yarrow prefers to lie fallow in the wilderness, being spotted by only an educated few who know of its incredible, glamorous history.

In its native lands yarrow has fallen in and out of fashion as a healing plant for centuries, and there's evidence that people have put it to use for sixty thousand years, stretching back to the time of the Neanderthals. This must have proven tiresome for yarrow, and maybe this is why the plant chose to reject civilization. The ancient Chinese method of foretelling the future, the I Ching, relies on dried yarrow stalks. Linnaeus wrote that Swedes once used yarrow instead of hops in brewing beer to increase its intoxication potential.

However yarrow's main usage is not symbolic or culinary but medicinal. As with many healing herbs, one wonders what happy (or unhappy) accident led to the plant's medicinal applications. Yarrow lends itself easily to such speculation. Because it spreads so rampantly in the wild, yarrow was probably growing in many old battlefields, and when soldiers were felled in war, their wounds would fortuitously brush against the plant. The plant's genus name, *Achillea,* is said to be a reference to Achilles's use of the plant to heal the wounds of his men battling in the Trojan War. Such usages also inspired the common name soldier's woundwort.

Culpeper reiterated this point in *The Complete Herball,* pointing out that the leaves of the plant were used as a poultice for wounds and that the plant could also be taken internally in the form of a decoction. He referred to it as "Militaris," presumably because of its service on the battlefield. The plant was actively used to treat wounds during the Civil War—remarkable when you consider its usage for the same purpose three thousand years before that by the Greeks. When Victorian ladies were creating the language of flowers, they assigned yarrow the meaning "war." Maybe yarrow is a strict pacifist and is just reacting to its Victorian-era association with war, because it was soon after that period that it went into hiding and was removed from the *Pharmacopoeia of the United States* list of healing plants, although the Shakers used it as a tonic well into this century and the Pah-Ute Indians used the plant in a decoction to treat weak stomachs.

And so, if you come upon yarrow in a field, merrily basking in the full sun it so loves and flourishing in a rich, well-drained soil, chuckling to itself as the days of summer grow longer, then shorter, and an entire season passes with its being left to its own devices, do take action. Educate yourself in how to tell yarrow from other plants. Seek out the strong, pleasant aroma, the pinnate leaves, and the flat-topped flowers. Bring along a field guide. If you have an interest in herbalism, harvest the plant.

There's also no reason why you shouldn't grow yarrow in your own garden border. As in the wild, it enjoys rich, well-drained soil and loves the sun. Yarrow also air-dries well, so if you can't quite muster the enthusiasm to take on herbalism, you can put yarrow into arrangements—a more creative choice than baby's breath. Although the appealing, open white flowers are beautiful, there are also some beautiful cultivars of different colors suited to this purpose. Yellow or pink flower heads are lovely, and even magenta types exist. Yarrow will add just the rustic, Old World touch you crave in your garden. Its wonderfully airy, fernlike foliage is as stunning as its flowers. So put yarrow back to work either medicinally or ornamentally in your home. Certainly the sabbatical has been long enough.

Yarrow and Plantain Salve

Yarrow is as useful in the medicine chest as it is in the garden. Pam Montgomery of Green Terrestrial "wildcrafts" yarrow—that is, she collects it from its natural setting—to use in her herbal medicinal preparations, shown at right. She stresses that fresh material should always be used for herbal preparations as it is more potent. The following topical salve recalls its antique use as a wound herb, when it went under the names soldier's woundwort and bloodwort. A variation is to add some vitamin E to boost its benefits to the skin or even to scent it with essential lavender oil at the point you add the beeswax. Keep in mind that some people are allergic to yarrow, so be aware of your sensitivities before using the salve.

Makes 1 pint

1 cup yarrow flowers
1 cup plantain leaves (Plantago major)
1 pint olive oil
beeswax

Harvest fresh yarrow and plantain. Fill 2 separate ½-pint jars with yarrow blossoms and plantain leaves. Add olive oil and stick in a knife or chopstick to stir the plant material a bit to ensure there are no air pockets. Place an airtight lid on the jars and allow the mixture to steep—out of the way of direct sunlight. The essence of the plants will infuse the oil. After 6 weeks, strain out the plants and reserve the oil in sterilized jars.

Transfer the flowers to cheesecloth and squeeze any additional oil from them into the jars. Then mix the oils from the two plants together in equal proportions.

Grate beeswax so it will melt quickly; place it in a pan with oil and very lightly heat it until it melts. Don't let it boil. Pour the beeswax into jars filled with oil. Add about 1 tablespoon grated beeswax to 3 ounces oil. This will create a smooth-textured salve to treat minor cuts and scrapes.

Aconitum napellus
MONKSHOOD
HELMET FLOWER
TURK'S-CAP

For those who are intrigued by the dark forces, own Ouija boards, and dabble in the tarot, monkshood is too good to miss. This is the quintessential plant of the occult, especially in the sense of the true meaning of the word, for monkshood's surreptitious form is hooded as if concealing something.

From the time of the ancient Greeks, monkshood has had a close association with evil. In Greek mythology Cerberus, the multiheaded dog with snakes for a tail, foamed at the mouth and imparted poison to the previously innocent aconite plant growing on the hill of Aconitus, at the gateway to Hades. Other Greek legends are heavily peppered with stories of fratricide and lovers avenging one another with monkshood.

In medieval-era legend in Germany the plant became heavily associated with the devil. Meanwhile, parallel legend in Norway linked this herb with Thor, the Norse god of thunder, earning it the name Thor-hat. In Holland, in association with an almost universally feared creature, it came to be known as wolf's wort. An ancient usage of the herb was to add the juice extracted from monkshood into a baited kill when stalking wolves, allowing the wolves to ingest it, although some historians have suggested that the reference to a wolf derives from Thor's battle with one. The shape of the flower naturally associated the plant with the cap of darkness, which in Icelandic myth allowed those who wore it to make themselves invisible. But later, when the Benedictine order became firmly established in Europe in the tenth century, their garments acted as inspiration for its most frequently used common name.

This intricate, layered belief system set the stage for monkshood's role in witch lore and witch trials, which began in the fifteenth century. Witchcraft was considered a heresy by Christians and the trials became a special form of entertainment in France, Germany, Scotland, England, and Italy.

In his *Lycanthropy, Metamorphosis, and Ecstasy of Witches,* published in 1615, Jean de Nynauld neatly explained basic witch ointments and their uses. There was the ointment of the imagination, which would put the witch in contact with the "other side". Among other ghastly ingredients not fit to be mentioned here, de Nynauld listed monkshood, mixed with the juice of water parsnip, cinquefoil, deadly nightshade, and soot. A dosage of this, he contended, was enough to put a woman into a "sabbatical" state in which she would be in two places—one physical, the other mental—simultaneously.

The philosopher Henry More explained in 1653 how such a magic ointment, applied to the body, would work: by "filling the pores, [it] keeps out the cold and keeps in the heat and spirits." Therefore, he reasoned, the soul could be free to flit about while the body kept warm so the two could be united as if nothing happened.

Another ointment was, of course, flying ointment, which created the sensations of riding. To the typical question in a witch trial "How is the ointment with which you rub your broomstick made?" the accused witch, after much baiting, would probably produce an account involving monkshood and belladonna. The witches also, it was well known, regularly poisoned people, and they used monkshood in their deadly ointments, along with hemlock, poplar leaves, and soot. In the Middle Ages, not understanding how diseases were transmitted, people even fingered the witches' killing ointments in outbreaks of plague.

More than a century after the witch trials ended, a medical experimenter named Otto Snell recorded in 1891 his own experiments with the types of drug combinations cited by de Nynauld; Snell's research led the way for academics who studied witchcraft. Snell concluded that the only effect of the drugs was a headache.

Snell either erred in his ingredients or had stumbled on something never again repeated, because monkshood, especially in combination with belladonna, is a most powerful drug. It is no wonder that the herbs cited in the witch trials were thought to produce the incredible results stated: monkshood's effect on the heart and the drugged state brought about by belladonna were a heady combination.

Bringing new meaning to the expression "dressed to kill," monkshood is garbed in flowers, leaves, and roots that look appealing but conceal a deadly toxin. The stunning violet flowers are like Snow White's apple: they contain a poison as powerful as their beauty. Some people have even been fooled by the leaves of the plant into thinking it is wild parsley and by the roots into thinking it is horseradish. Although the plant is a member of the buttercup family, Ranunculaceae, don't be misled by these cheerful, carefree associations. All parts of monkshood, particularly the root, yield a substance that contains toxic alkaloids. These slow the heart and decrease blood pressure; it is said that when applied to the skin, monkshood numbs pain; liniments containing monkshood have been used to relieve neuralgia and rheumatism. A relative that also goes by the name aconite, *A. carmichaeli,* is much used in Chinese herbal medicine as a "warming" drug for the same

Monkshood, opposite above, prepares to bloom in the herb garden of a four-hundred-year-old farmhouse and ironically enough, former nunnery. The plant dazzles in full, velvety flower at Wisley Garden, opposite below.

effect. But in Western herbal medicine this drug is considered too toxic to handle, legitimate though its healing powers may be.

No one would have accused nineteenth-century doctors of witchcraft, but concoctions strongly resembling flying and killing ointments were prescribed regularly in that era—when the malefaction of witchcraft was far enough in the past not to produce suspicious associations. As late as 1903 a prescription in the *Pharmacopoeia of the Royal Infirmary of Edinburgh* for a combination of drugs that if taken two centuries earlier would have had you burned at the stake, was simply prescribed matter-of-factly as a liniment. The combination for a "Linimenta" was a mixture of equal parts of

"Aconite Liniment, Belladonna Liniment, and Chloroform Liniment." According to the book, the liniment was to be used "in rheumatic and superficial pains, etc."

One would not want to sit and ponder the results of such blithe prescriptions for long. But from the time we are children, we are all drawn to the things we are supposed to avoid. So who could fight the otherworldly forces and not grow this magical herb?

If you are spellbound by monkshood, by all means grow it in your garden. But if there are little children about, best err on the side of caution and wait until they've grown. Because it requires rich soil and some shade, it is best to separate the plant from dry-soil-loving herbs.

Althaea officinalis
MARSH MALLOW
Althaea rosea
HOLLYHOCK

The hollyhock is the peasant's rose. Spires of hollyhock blooming about the gateway typify the classic, lovingly tended British cottage garden. In medieval times, while the gentry adorned their walled, meticulously tended gardens with roses, lilies, and other aristocratic plants, commoners happily cultivated the humble hollyhock in the disarray of their cottage gardens. Although the hollyhock has been likened to the rose—past misnomers include Outlandish Rose and *Rosa ultramarina*—the gangly, rustic flowers make it less majestic than the rose but twice as endearing.

As with so many other heirloom flowers, the hollyhock was most likely introduced to Europe during the time of the Crusades. It originally came from China, where the flower buds and leaves had been eaten for a millennium as a salad herb before the plant was brought to the Continent. There are references to the "holy-hocke" in a garden poem dating from at least the mid–fifteenth century, but the hollyhock's common name is an enigma. Some people say that its association with the Crusades made it known as a "holy" flower and that *hoc*, the Anglo-Saxon word for mallow, was simply tacked on. Another theory reasons that hollyhock derives from "holy-oak," because the plant grows so high—to nine feet—that it was likened to an oak. In his herbal, John Parkinson refers to the hollyhock's "tall branches, like Trees." At any rate, it's established that the genus name, *Althaea,* is Greek for marsh mallow.

Wherever it grows, the hollyhock is a sentimental favorite of the people. So beloved was the hollyhock by the American colonists that they brought seeds with them from England to the New World. Cheerful turrets of hollyhocks brightened up the settlers' often bleak lives, rising above their fences and peeking into their windows. By the time of the American Revolution the hollyhock had become such a staple that George Washington insisted on growing the flower on his Mount Vernon grounds.

The mallow family—to which hollyhock belongs—is a varied lot, but all members tend to have large, beautiful flowers. Like cotton, its well-known mallow cousin, the hollyhock has been used to produce fibers similar to flax. Hollyhock was an important entry in both John Parkinson's and John Gerard's famous herbals; they valued the hollyhock for sundry medicinal purposes. Three centuries later on another continent, the Shakers used the hollyhock to correct coughs and "weakness in females."

The hollyhock's esteemed European cousin, *A. officinalis,* the true marsh mallow, was valued in the past more for its usefulness than its looks. This plant's roots yield a gelatinous substance that was used to bind the marshmallow confection in the past (now replaced by gelatin). Also referred to as sweetweed, this plant grows to about half of the hollyhock's height and has pretty pinkish flowers. It grows wild in marshes in the eastern United States, where it is an escapee from the garden and dons large rosy pink flowers in July and August.

Consider bringing the hollyhock into your garden for a touch of living history. All you need is ordinary garden soil and a sunny location to grow this showy mallow.

At the Shaker Garden in Old Chatham, New York, tall spires of hollyhock, false indigo, flax, roses, and mints grow, left.

Calendula officinalis
CALENDULA
POT MARIGOLD

Cultivating calendula in your garden is like inviting a dear old friend for an extended visit during the entire warm-weather season. Not at all concerned with SPFs, calendula follows the sun and probably won't even acknowledge your invitation unless you guarantee plenty of it. So from the moment you sow seeds in April or May, make sure an abundance of sunlight is shining down to speed the plant's journey.

Like any good friend, calendula is not a passive guest and helps out around the house. Although her charming presence is always delightful in a flower arrangement, she also knows how to be handy in social situations. Calendula brightens up dinner conversation by her mere presence. When you have to have the boss over for dinner and the conversation turns flat, run and grab calendula—arrange her petals and leaves in a salad or strew this versatile flower's petals on rice. She will instantly spark conversation when the boss wonders who this charming addition to the dinner party is.

Perhaps calendula's most unusual asset is her remarkable knowledge of country cures. In salve form this helpful plant treats cuts, burns, and rashes, coming to the rescue in summertime after you have been on a long, demanding hike or have been out working in the garden and have been scraped by rose or bramble bushes. Don't be

A Proper Newe Booke of Cokerye, published during England's Tudor period, called for a "tarte of marygoldes, primroses, or cowslips." Pot-marigold flowers, opposite, were the intended ingredient, but the plant has medicinal as well as culinary virtues.

shocked if your good friend calendula also takes easily to vodka or gin; when used in a tincture with these liquors this wonder flower is thought to aid in stomach ailments. Calendula even purports to cure warts with the juice from her blossoms. Calendula flowers are also used to bring golden highlights to the hair.

Calendula is famous for her other, more esoteric attributes as well. It is thought that if she grows in your lover's footsteps, he or she will remain faithful. Some people also believe that she can predict the future,

claiming that if you place blossoms under your pillow, your dreams will be prophetic.

You will be saddened to see calendula close up her petals and make preparations to depart at the end of the summer, but you can prolong her visit by the cut-and-come-again method: pinch the flower head off the stem, and the plant will keep blooming and may even be induced to stay through the first few frosts and perhaps even a light snowfall. However calendula must draw the line somewhere and take her leave. She is an annual plant; you will have to sow seeds in spring the next season.

But don't despair. Remember that her name, calendula, comes from the ancient Roman word *calends,* which means the first of every month, a reference to her long blooming period, being in the garden throughout most of the year. Rest assured, constant calendula will keep in touch throughout the winter. To ensure her presence, dry her petals by spreading them out on paper. After they have dried, pulverize them by rubbing them through your palms and pour the contents into a sterilized airtight jar. When winter's chill lowers your spirits and the sound of the raging wind outdoors makes you long for summer, plop calendula's blossoms into steaming hot soup or stew, and you will be comforted instantly.

Calendula Oil

Herbalist Pam Montgomery of Green Terrestrial in Milton, New York, makes a massage oil from calendula harvested from her spirally shaped herb garden on the banks of the Hudson River. The oil, shown at left, is wonderful for massaging the body and for treating skin irritations. She recommends using olive oil for herbal preparations because it will not turn rancid and is easily absorbed into the skin. No measurements are given because you simply fill whatever size jar you have available with calendula blossoms, then add as much olive oil as will fit.

calendula blossoms
olive oil (any kind, but Pam prefers imported)

Harvest fresh calendula. Fill a sterilized jar full with blossoms. Add olive oil and stick in a knife or chopstick to stir the blossoms a bit to ensure there are no air pockets. Place an airtight lid on the jar and allow the mixture to steep out of the way of direct sunlight. The essence of the flowers will infuse the oil. After 6 weeks, strain out the flowers and use the remaining oil.

Chamaemelum nobile
ROMAN CHAMOMILE
Matricarea recutita
GERMAN CHAMOMILE

Although Roman chamomile could easily take a haughty stance and brag that it has graced the lawns of the finest estates and castles of the world, it is not a class-conscious or snobbish herb. The species has been known to grow wild in the most unpretentious of places, such as in the British cottage garden and in the back hills of the American South. This herb's split personality has been intensified by another matter: two species lay claim to being the true chamomile. In a situation similar to that of pennyroyal—whose common name refers to separate American and European plants—chamomile is the catchall name for two plants that look alike and have similar usages. Both Roman and German chamomile have individual merit, however, so there's no need to sow dissension.

Chamaemelum nobile, Roman chamomile, is a low-growing perennial plant, the type used for lawns by the Elizabethans. It grows tidily in garden areas that can't be mown, such as between flagstones and around the legs of old stone benches. *C. nobile* 'Treneague' is particularly useful for this purpose. It doesn't flower but has a delicious apple scent and is very compact.

Plants and people are one and the same to Roman chamomile as far as its medicinal benefits are concerned. This herb purportedly restores vigor to neighboring plants, which may be a result of its insect-repellent qualities. Or it could simply be that the plant's cheerful, fragrant, daisylike flowers enhance their surroundings to the

extent that everything around it looks better. Roman chamomile also heals and improves the appearance of people. In tea form it has long been used to treat stomach and head disorders, and we all know chamomile tea's applications from Beatrix Potter's story *Peter Rabbit.* It is one of the ancient secrets of European blondes—the flowers used as a hair rinse intensify blonde highlights, although some people maintain that German chamomile better serves this purpose.

Roman chamomile also had medieval household applications as a strewing herb—when thrown on the floor in the house, it scented the air and repelled insects. To achieve the same effect, you need only to dry the flowers for potpourri. Try also air-drying the flowers for informal arrangements, perhaps complemented by a few wildflowers.

Classic British herbals usually list German chamomile, *Matricarea recutita,* as a weed. If the author was feeling magnanimous, this annual plant might have received the name "wild chamomile."

Despite this second-class status in the British Isles, this species is regarded in pockets of northern Europe as being the true chamomile. The dried flowers of German chamomile have traditionally been used by Germanic peoples as a tisane—a beverage of infused herbs—to aid digestion and insomnia. Linnaeus gave German chamomile the species name *chamomilla,* and he would have been pleased that the name, now outmoded, still creeps onto the plant labels of perfectly respectable botanic gardens. Since there is an old belief that Balder, the Norse god of light, took a special shine to the chamomile flower—known colloquially in the past in Scandinavia as Balder's eyelashes—we can assume that it is the *Matricaria* species. This plant, which grows taller than Roman chamomile and has daisylike flowers that are less perfumed, was often gathered along with other flowers on Midsummer Eve and made into culinary wreaths; cottagers would pluck the plant as needed for use as a medicinal tonic tea.

In keeping with their cheerful appearance, Roman and German chamomile enjoy sun. They can be grown from seed, but you'll get faster results from Roman chamomile if you propagate it from offshoots of an existing plant. Both chamomiles deserve a place in the herb garden, but if you have room for only one, let the style of the garden be your guide. For formality Roman chamomile should serve you well on account of its uniform, mosslike appearance. German chamomile is much more willing to let down its guard, and its brightly smiling, rustic flowers are never out of place in a sprawling, natural-looking herb garden.

An old British saying goes, "A good Coke [cook] is half a physycyon. For the chefe physycke . . . doth come from the Kytchyn." The Late Victorian Pharmacy in Edinburgh adheres to this philosophy in its displays, opposite. Apothecaries would often obtain fresh plants, such as German chamomile, above, and dry them for professional use.

Chamomile is today used much the same way it has been employed for centuries. Dora Gerber of Swissette Herb Farm in New York State is the author of these pleasant chamomile recipes, meant to soothe and relax.

Aromatic Meadow Tea

Three marvelous herbs scent this aromatic tea. Chamomile produces calming effects and also soothes the stomach. Some cultures even believe that it can prevent aging. Another ingredient of this tea, catnip, exhilarates cats but has the opposite effect on humans. People feel drowsy, even somewhat sedated, after drinking it, which explains why it has been used to treat hysteria. Marjoram, too, has a sweet, mellow taste that adds to the complex pleasantness of the tea. Add mint to this tea for a livelier flavor.

Makes 3½ ounces

1¼ ounces chamomile flowers
    (Chamaemelum nobile)
¾ ounce catnip (Nepeta cataria)
1 ounce sweet marjoram (Origanum
    Majorana)
½ ounce mint (Mentha spp.)
Combine herbs in airtight container.

For 1 cup of tea, pour a cup of boiling water over 2 teaspoons of herb blend and steep for 5 to 10 minutes. Strain and drink warm.

Chamaemelum nobile 'Treneague' doesn't flower and releases an apple scent when trod on, making it a lovely choice for the scent garden at Hatfield House, right. Centifolia and gallica roses bloom nearby.

Soothing Mealtime Tea

To make the best herbal tea possible, allow plenty of time for it to steep. Unlike traditional teas, herbal teas do not become darker as they steep, but take on a light green, yellow, or amber coloration that does not intensify in appearance but does in taste. This soothing medicinal tea is naturally green and aids digestion; it's also good for easing stomach problems. Drink 1 cup before a meal or after eating. It has a somewhat bitter taste, but resist adding sugar; the idea is not a dessert tea but a medicinal one. Use air-dried herbs for the tea and shake the mixture before use.

Makes 3 ounces

½ ounce chamomile flowers (Chamaemelum nobile)
1 ounce wormwood (Artemisia absinthium)
1 ounce European centaury (Erythraea centaurium)
½ ounce mint (Mentha piperita)
Combine herbs in airtight container.

For 1 cup of tea, pour 1 cup boiling water over 2 teaspoons herb blend and steep for 5 to 10 minutes. Strain and drink warm.

Herbal Aromatic Treatment

Whether you are experiencing the effects of a cold or simply need the lift provided by pleasing scents, try this chamomile blend.

Makes about 2 ounces

¾ ounce sage (Salvia officinalis)
¾ ounce chamomile (Chamaemelum nobile)
⅓ ounce thyme (Thymus serpyllum)

Put 2 tablespoons mixed herbs in a large bowl and add 1 quart boiling water. Lean over and breathe in the mixture, trapping the herbal steam by placing a towel or cloth over your head and extending to the bowl. Continue to do so for 10 minutes.

Lunaria annua
HONESTY
MONEY PLANT

In the days when medicine was as much a product of folklore as it was of science, those persons suffering from madness, thought to be influenced by the phases of the moon, were given a seemingly logical cure for their ills: a dosage of *Lunaria annua*. The botanical name for this plant refers to the seedpods, which become luminous as the plant ages and resemble a brightly shining moon. Because of lunaria's appearance, it seemed to follow that the quirky-looking herb could counteract giddiness brought on by the constant waxing and waning of the dotty old moon.

When it eventually became clear that no amount of lunaria could cure moonstruck madness, the plant was retired as a medicinal herb but taken up as an everlasting to decorate the home. When dry the pods' valves fall off, revealing a silvery, radiant interior, which has inspired disparate common names. Some people prefer to call lunaria by its endearing name "honesty," inspired by the manner in which the satiny white pods reveal themselves when dried. More businesslike types think of lunaria as "money plant" and "silver shilling," since it does resemble currency when dried.

It became very popular in the eighteenth century to dry the plant for use in winter decorations, and in the following century the Victorians (who always took to unusual-looking plants) combined lunaria with dried hydrangea and other dramatic plants in their enormous arrangements.

Lunaria is still beloved, but in this century it has actually inspired a form of dementia. There are people who insist on dyeing the dried plant in a variety of colors

to "improve" its appearance. Do not let yourself succumb to this madness. It's much nicer to keep things simple and work with the plant's own natural dried color. And, by all means, do not relegate it to the role of "filler" in an arrangement. All too often lunaria is used as an afterthought in floral designs, a terrible slight to this ancient plant. To give lunaria its due, dust off your Culpeper and look up a few plants that herbalists once believed were governed by the moon—poppy, loosestrife, and the white rose, among them—and create a lunar arrangement, using all-dried or fresh and dried flowers. Consider honoring the phases of the moon by throwing a full-moon party, using the pristine pods of lunaria as your decoration. For such an occasion you might drape the pods over a mantelpiece, hang them over doorways, mistletoe fashion, or decorate a bedside table with them as a charming cure for insomnia.

In your dried arrangements using lunaria, avoid baby's breath, strawflowers, eucalyptus, and other visual clichés and combine the dear old plant with some of the less traditional everlastings: gauzy pasque flower seed heads, spiky sea hollies, and the Gladwin iris *(Iris foetidissima),* a long-lived dried plant whose seed capsules split open to reveal orange and scarlet seeds. Don't forget that fresh lunaria is absolutely beautiful in arrangements; its lively green color combines vividly with red flowers, and the little point at the edge of the seedpods adds a flourish to floral designs.

Lunaria was also widely cultivated in the past because it was thought to have the power to bewitch. It was believed that simply looking upon the plant in the moonlight would enable you to become transformed into an aerial being. Lunaria is still, of course, a magical plant, but this is

Although it has origins in the medicinal realm, honesty, left, is now merely symbolic in the healing herb garden. Long ago, its roots were eaten and its leaves combined with other plants to make a salve for wounds. For everlasting arrangements, harvest when the seedpod is fully formed.

simply on account of its beauty. The English writer William Robinson, who advocated an unfussy, natural garden style, advocated lunaria in his classic *The Wild Garden* for its ease of cultivation and its looks. He wrote that lunaria is "one of the best plants for naturalization" and that it "is one of the prettiest plants in early summer." You don't even have to wait for the seedpods to reveal their inner white section before harvesting the plant; when the seedpods turn brown, pick the plant by the stem and remove the valves yourself. Even if you are not inclined to use the plant in arrangements, you will take delight in lunaria throughout the seasons. Its fragrant lilac flowers bloom in midsummer, and the seedpods reveal themselves in autumn, glinting eerily under the full hunter's moon of October, and may even continue to cling on into winter.

Two inspired herbal creations, created by Tage Anderson of Copenhagen, display fresh and dried honesty. Opposite, fresh honesty combines pleasingly with roses and pinks, two herbal flowers whose petals have brightened meals for centuries. A cream-colored topiary of dried honesty, right, makes an unusual holiday tabletop decoration.

Ranunculus acris
BUTTERCUP
MEADOW CROWFOOT

One of the greatest discoveries of archaeological science was a woolly mammoth, perfectly preserved due to being quickly frozen. It was found in a half-standing, half-kneeling position on the Bersovk River in Siberia. What confused scientists at first was how the animal came to be so quickly frozen when it had been in the process of feasting on *Ranunculus acris,* the buttercup. The scientists studying the strange phenomenon reasoned that buttercups grow in temperate conditions and dote on sun, so the mammoth could not have been frozen by a winter chill. The theory goes that an unprecedented catastrophic explosion under the earth produced a strange chilling wind that froze everything in its path.

The mammoth dining on ancient buttercups did not meet its end from poisoning from them, but people very well could. Even Nicholas Culpeper was conservative when writing about this herb: "This fiery and hot-spirited herb of Mars is no way fit to be given inwardly." He felt, however, that an "ointment of the leaves or flowers" might be safe for some complaints. Two hundred years later, the Shakers put the herb to use gingerly, acknowledging that it could produce a violent reaction and was too acrid to be used internally, especially when fresh. They recommended it for external application to skin irritations.

The buttercup does appear in modern herbalism texts, but with the warning that the fresh plant can be poisonous. It is usually recommended that the plant be used dried and powdered and only under medical supervision to promote healing of wounds.

Unless you are herbally trained and know precisely what you are doing, it is best to let buttercup take its place among other medicinal plants in your garden—foxglove, monkshood, and henbane, to name a few—that once had a plethora of common usages but today are merely symbolic of the grand and complex tradition in which herb gardeners are participating.

Instead, put this flower to another historic usage. In describing the plant in his *The Complete Herball,* Culpeper remarked approvingly, "I do not remember that I ever saw any thing yellower." It's such a pretty plant that you may wish to use it in flower arrangements. The common varieties found growing in the field are beautiful and belong in wispy wildflower arrangements with dock, purple loosestrife, field grasses, heather, and other unfussy plants. In the seventeenth century, European florists began to carry *Ranunculus* at their shops, and they became great favorites for domestic use. While people were aware of their herbal applications, they were more likely to festoon their homes with buttercup blooms—ignoring peasant folklore claiming that smelling them would drive you mad, hence the old British colloquial name "insane." As a result, double-flowered varieties have been developed, and these are very handsome in the garden as well as in flower arrangements. They are especially lovely grouped with other distinctive-looking plants in the Ranunculaceae family, such as monkshood and delphinium, whose bluish lavender colors will contrast pleasantly with the sunny yellow blooms.

For centuries, herbalists have built up their health with buttercup, right. Gerard believed that if ranunculus is "hanged in a linnen cloth about the necke of him that is lunatike in waine of the moone, then he shall forthwith be cured."

APPENDIX

SOURCES
BIBLIOGRAPHY
INDEX

SOURCES

All sources are mail order unless otherwise noted; call or write for their catalogs; where possible, catalog prices are noted.

Herb Plants and Seeds

Abundant Life Seed Foundation
P.O. Box 772
Port Townsend, WA 98368
(206) 385-5660 general information
(206) 385-7192 to order seeds
nonprofit organization offers seeds of native North American herbs and those of North Temperate Zone, including nasturtiums, sunflowers, chia, basils, borage, poppy, lamb's quarters, clary sage, yarrows, foxglove, hollyhock, and rugosa rose

J. S. Akin
P.O. Box 6
Sibley, LA 71073
(318) 377-3653
culinary bay tree stock

Alpine Valley Gardens
2627 Calistoga Road
Santa Rosa, CA 95404
(707) 575-3122
carries daylily bulbs, a Chinese culinary herb

Camelot North
R.R. 2, Box 398
Pequot Lakes, MN 56472
(218) 568-8922
selection of culinary herb plants, including mints, lemon balm, basil, and sage; catalog costs $1; garden open to public at selected times

Caprilands Herb Farm
534 Silver Street
Coventry, CT 06238
(203) 742-7244
plants and seeds, including numerous *Allium* species, lavenders, mints, oreganos, upright and prostrate rosemaries, culinary and creeping thymes, angelica, catnip, lovage, hyssop, bee balm, sweet rocket, yarrows; also has extensive selection of herbal crafts, such as scented wreaths, rosebud balls, and lavender sachets; pilgrimages made from all over Northeast to visit famous display gardens

Casa Yerba Gardens
3459 Days Creek Road
Days Creek, OR 97429
general selection of herb seeds; plants available in spring and autumn

Catnip Acres Farm
67 Christian Street
Oxford, CT 06483-1224
(203) 888-5649
wide selection of herb plants, including angelica, borage, lemon balm, hyssop, foxglove, and yarrow; garden open to public by special appointment

Companion Plants
7247 North Coolville Ridge Road
Athens, OH 45701
(614) 592-4643
herb plants and seeds, with emphasis on native North American woodland plants, including goldenseal and ginseng; also carries dye plants and general selection of herbs, including foxglove, henbane, greater celandine, calendula, pennyroyals, and lavender; catalog costs $2; garden open to public at selected times

Comstock, Ferre & Co.
P.O. Box 125
263 Main Street
Wethersfield, CT 06109
(203) 529-3319
herb and everlastings seeds, with mix of old-fashioned species and new varieties; catalog costs $1; garden open to public at selected times

The Cook's Garden
P.O. Box 65
Moffitt's Bridge
Londonderry, VT 05148-0065
(802) 824-3400
culinary herb seeds, with acclaimed varieties of oregano and basil, including a large-leaved 'Mammoth' basil that can be used for stuffing poultry and wrapping foods; special dandelion salad green varieties also carried

Cricket Hill Herb Farm Ltd.
Glen Street
Rowley, MA 01969
(508) 948-2818
emphasis on culinary herb plants and seeds, including 30 varieties of mint, 20 varieties of thyme, and variegated-leaf plants; also carry culinary herb blends and potpourri ingredients; catalog costs $1; garden open to public at selected times

Crownsville Nursery
P.O. Box 797
Crownsville, MD 21032
(301) 923-2212
general selection of herb plants and perennial flowers, including daylilies; catalog is constantly updated and costs $2

Dabney Herbs
P.O. Box 22061
Louisville, KY 40222
(502) 893-5198
unusual selection of herb plants changes often; includes dye herbs such as woad and agrimony; also carries native North American medicinal herbs, including bloodroot, black cohosh, sumac, and elder; hollyhock, sunflower, and yarrows also in stock

Ecology Action:

Bountiful Gardens
19550 Walker Road
Willits, CA 95490
mail-order branch of Ecology Action sells herb seeds, including salad rocket, Roman and German chamomiles, calendula, Good King Henry, mullein, coriander, sunflower, nasturtium, Welsh onion, wormwood, sorrel, and rue; also carries bath herbs, natural insect controls

Common Ground Garden Supply
2225 El Camino Road
Palo Alto, CA 94306
(415) 328-6752
retail shop of Ecology Action sells herb plants and seeds

The Flowery Branch
4511 T. Moore Road
Oakwood, GA 30566
(404) 536-8380
over 450 varieties of herb seeds, including dye and medicinal plants; two-year catalog costs $2

Fox Hill Farm
P.O. Box 9
440 West Michigan Avenue
Parma, MI 49269
(517) 531-3179
selection of 400 types of herb plants in culinary, medicinal, dye, fiber, everlasting, perfume, and insect repellent/attractant categories; best known for 20 varieties of basil, topiary herbs (rosemary, bay, lavender, basil), robust mugwort, and moss-lined culinary herb baskets

Kingfisher Incorporated/
Halcyon Gardens
P.O. Box 75
Wexford, PA 15090
(412) 935-2233
herb seeds, with special collections of packaged herb blends, including Herb Seed Collection for different garden styles: Colonial Kitchen, Gourmet Salad, Fragrant, and Shakespeare Theme; also carries Kitchensill Garden, Herb Nursery Kits, Perfect Herbs for Cats blends

The Herb Barn
P.O. Box 31
Bodine, PA 17722
(717) 995-9327
general selection of over 125 herb plants

Le Jardin du Gourmet
P.O. Box 75
St. Johnsbury Center, VT 05863
(802) 684-2201
culinary herb plants and seeds, including angelica, *Allium* species, lemon balm, basils, borage, catnip, chives, genuine French dandelion seeds; dill, fennel, and poppies; Roman and German chamomiles, lavender, pennyroyal, and honesty; bouquet garni, herb vinegars.

Johnny's Selected Seeds
Foss Hill Road
Albion, ME 04910
(207) 437-9294
selection of culinary herb seeds, from basil to watercress, grown with emphasis on organic methods; also offers poppies, sunflowers, *Violas,* Shirley poppies, nasturtium, and natural insecticides

Le Marché Seeds International
450 Porter Street
Dixon, CA 95620
European and Southeast Asian culinary herb seeds and French Potager seed mix sold at retail store (products also carried nationally by specialty shops)

Meadowbrook Herb Garden
Route 138
Wyoming, RI 02898
(401) 539-7603
selection of culinary seeds, as well as mugwort, chamomile, and lavender; also offers dried culinary herbs, syrups, and herbal cosmetics

Nichols Garden Nursery, Inc.
1190 North Pacific Highway
Albany, OR 97321
(503) 928-9280
selection of herb seeds and plants, including lavender, basil, and Oriental herbs; essential oils and potpourri supplies also available

Pinetree Garden Seeds
Route 100
New Gloucester, ME 04260
(207) 926-3400
emphasis on culinary herb seeds, including basils, nasturtium, chervil, coriander, and fennel; some perennial herb plants available in spring; everlastings, including honesty and lamb's ears, poppies, *Violas,* hollyhock, and hyssop

Plants of the Southwest
930 Baca Street
Santa Fe, NM 87501
(505) 983-1548
seeds and plants, including lamb's quarters, peppergrass, basils, borage, lovage, chives, German chamomile, nasturtium, cilantro, sage, and parsley; Mexican/Southwestern herbs include epazote (*Chenopodium* relative of lamb's quarters)

Roses of Yesterday & Today
802 Brown's Valley Road
Watsonville, CA 95076-0398
(408) 724-3537
230 varieties of rose shrubs

Sandy Mush Herb Nursery
Route 2, Surrett Cove Road
Leicester, NC 28748
(704) 683-2014
perennial plants and annual seeds, including scented geraniums, thymes, mints, artemisias, and lavenders; catalog costs $4

Seeds Blum
Idaho City Stage
Boise, ID 83706
(208) 342-0858
selection of seeds

Shepherd's Garden Seeds
6116 Highway 9
Felton, CA 95018
(408) 335-5311
culinary herb seeds, including basils

Smith Creek Greenhouse
Smith Creek Road
Raymond, WA 98577
plants and full range of herbal household and culinary gifts sold only on premises, grown by Bears, Herbs, Hearts & Flowers (see "Household, Cosmetic, and Healthful Herbal Gifts")

Taylor's Herb Garden, Inc.
1535 Lone Oak Road
Vista, CA 92083
(619) 727-3485
mostly culinary herb plants and seedlings; lavenders and thyme groundcovers; catalog costs $1

Well-Sweep Herb Farm
317 Mount Bethel Road
Port Murray, NJ 07865
(201) 852-5390
wide and unusual selection of plants and seeds includes monkshood, *Allium* species, artemisias (including mugwort), over 20 basils, bay, bee balm, borage, Roman and German chamomiles, American and European pennyroyals, clovers, mints, lavenders, feverfew, hops, horseradish, violets, over 10 yarrows, about 40 varieties of rosemary, 30 sages, and over 50 thymes; also carries dried decorative herbs and fragrant herb blends; catalog costs $1; garden open to public at selected times

Culinary Herbal Gifts

Blanchard & Blanchard & Son
P.O. Box 1080
Norwich, VT 05055
802-295-9200
preservative-free salad dressings, including Lemon-Mustard with Dill, Poppyseed, Honey Mustard with Tarragon, Tomato-Basil, Tomato-Dill, Garlic, and Northern Italian; also carries Rosemary Marinade and Tangy Lemon Marinade (seasoned with herbs)

Chicama Vineyards
Stoney Hill Road
West Tisbury, MA 02575
(508) 693-0309
25 herb vinegars, in such combinations as Parsley, Sage, Rosemary and Thyme; Lemon-Chive; Chive and Cracked Peppercorn; Basil and Garlic in red-wine vinegar; Opal Basil; and Rosemary; also carries oils (Moroccan, Cajun, and Thai) flavored with herbs and spices

Di Camillo Baking Company Inc.
811 Linwood Ave.
Niagara Falls, NY 14305
(800) 634-4363
flatbread with poppy seeds; dry focaccia flatbread with black pepper and poppyseed; cheesebreads with herbal blends; breadcrumbs seasoned with chives, garlic, basil, and oregano; tomato breadsticks seasoned with pepper, basil, and parsley; herb bread with black pepper, poppyseed, and parsley; *biscotti al formaggio* (cheese crisps) seasoned with herbs

Ethel M Chocolates
P.O. Box 98505
Las Vegas, NV 89193-9968
(800) 634-6584
mint truffles and mint coins made with natural ingredients

Hattie's Kitchen
Old Post Road
Bowdoinham, ME 04008
(207) 666-8827
Spicy Dilled Green Beans; gift packs
available

The Herb & Spice Collection
P.O. Box 118, D18
Norway, IA 52318
(800) 365-4372
culinary herbs and spices as well as
herbal teas and oils; also carries
potpourris and body-care products

The Herbfarm
32804 Issaquah-Fall City Road
Fall City, WA 98024
(206) 784-2222
numerous herb culinary (including
vinegars, teas, wreaths), craft, pet-care,
and body-care gifts change seasonally;
plant mail-order list costs $2.50; garden
open to public at selected times

Herb Gathering, Inc.
Forget-Me-Nots Division/Paula
Winchester
5742 Kenwood Avenue
Kansas City, MO 64110
(816) 523-2653
gift baskets of fresh-cut culinary herbs
and herbal crafts; send SASE requesting
Forget-Me-Nots flier

Hilltop Herb Farm
P.O. Box 325
Romayor, TX 77368
(713) 592-5859
herbally based jams, jellies, chutneys,
relishes, teas, and gift baskets; also
carries plants and seeds

The Hough Bakery
1519 Lakeview Road
Cleveland, OH 44112
(216) 795-0600
famous Poppyseed Dressing available at
store only

Kelchner's
114 Elephant Road
Box 245
Dublin, PA 18917
(215) 249-3439
(215) 249-3358
freshly ground horseradish—not a sauce
base—used to make Kelchner's
Horseradish, Hot Cocktail Sauce, Hot
Mustard, and Horseradish with Red
Beets

Livingston Farms
2224 Livingston Road
St. John's, MI 48879
(517) 224-3616
(517) 224-6685
peppermint and spearmint oils

Lowelands Farm
Route 1
Box 98
Middleburg, VA 22117
(703) 687-6923
Herbal Honeys and Herbal Wine Vinegars

Paula's California Herb Vinegars and
Premium Oils
Sweet Adelaide Enterprises, Inc.
3457-A South La Cienega Boulevard
Los Angeles, CA 90016
(213) 559-6196
herb vinegars include Best Salad (cider
vinegar, mint, dill, and garlic), Italian
Garden (red wine vinegar, oregano, bay
leaf, and garlic), and Fiesta (apple cider
vinegar, cilantro, and chili pepper); low-
sodium herb seasonings include Fish
Seasoning (with dill and spices), Poultry
Seasoning (with tarragon and spices),
Beef Seasoning (with garlic, pepper and
spices), and Lamb Seasoning (with
rosemary and spices)

Rathdowney Herbs and Herb Crafts
3 River Street
Bethel, VT 05032
(800) 543-8885
(802) 234-9928, in Vermont
culinary herbal-spice blends; herbal soup
mixes and pancake mixes; also carries
herbal potpourris and wreaths; herbal
carpet freshener; pet repellents (to keep
them away from plants, furniture, etc.)

Rowena's
758 West 22nd Street
Norfolk, VA 23517
(800) 627-8699
Blue Crab Bay Seafood Marinade (an
herbed marinade or dressing), Dried
Tomato and Chive Olive Oil, Mariner's
Sauce (an herbal sauce)

The Sunflower Cafe
Main Street
Grace City, ND 58445
(701) 674-3159
fresh sunflower seeds available through
mail order; special arrangements can be
made to ship regionally renowned
Sunflower Pie

United Society of Shakers
Sabbathday Lake
Poland, Spring, ME 04274
(207) 926-4597
dried culinary herbs, used both singly
and in mixes; latest blends in tins are
Dill Dip, Salad Seasoning, and Poultry
Seasoning; dried herbs now also
available in smaller polybags; also
carries unusual selection of herbal teas,
herb vinegars, and aromatic herbal
potpourris; send legal-size SASE to
receive catalog

W. S. Wells & Sons
P.O. Box 109
Wilton, ME 04294
(207) 645-3393
Belle of Maine Canned Fiddleheads and
Dandelions

Household, Cosmetic, and Healthful Herbal Gifts

Baudelaire, Inc.
Forest Road
Marlow, NH 03456
(800) 327-2324
herbal bath oils, including Chamomile, Hops, Lavender, Melisse (balm mint), Rosemary, and Thyme; herbal soaps also available

Bears, Herbs, Hearts & Flowers
81 E. Raymond-Willapa Road
Raymond, WA 98577
(206) 942-2122
herbal perfumes, cosmetics, and body-care products, including Calendula Baby Cream; Herbal Mint Mask; essential oils and seasonings; everlastings; instructive newsletter; catalog costs $2

Bittersweet Farm
6294 Seville Road
Seville, OH 44273
(216) 887-5293
mail-order herb wreaths and herbal crafts; catalog costs $2; selection of herb plants (sold on premises only), including bay, hyssop, mugwort, rosemary, lavender, soapwort, loosestrife, hollyhock, foxglove, and poppies; garden open to public at selected times

C. F. Wolfe
378 West End Avenue
New York, NY 10024
(212) 362-6185
"Fleurpourri" preserved whole-flower-and-herb arrangements as well as herbs and dried flowers for potpourri; silica and essential oils for creating potpourri

The Cottage Herb Farm Shop
311 State Street
Albany, NY 12210
(518) 465-1130
retail farm shop sells herbal pillows, potpourri, teas, and sachets

The Faith Mountain Company
Main Street
P.O. Box 199
Sperryville, VA 22740
(703) 987-8824
(800) 822-7238
herbal potpourris and crafts, including wreaths, kissing balls, and corsages; shop also on premises; catalog costs $3

Frog Park Herbs
Waterville, NY 13480
(315) 841-8636
potpourri blends and supplies; wreaths; bath herb mixes; essential oils; also carries teas, culinary mixtures, and seeds

Hearts & Flowers By Ruth
P.O. Box 49
South Bend, WA 98586
rose and other herbal flower jewelry

Heaven's Herbal Creations
8202 West M.L. Avenue
Kalamazoo, MI 49009
(616) 375-2934
herbal cosmetics, custom scents, essential oils, body-care products—all created from organically grown herbs harvested on premises; shop also on premises as well as numerous gardens, including children's garden with herbal theme; catalog costs $2

Hedgehog Hill Farm
R.F.D. 2, Box 2010
Buckfield, ME 04220
(207) 388-2341
wreaths and wreath kits, bouquets, and arrangement kits; herbal vinegars, teas, and honeys; catalog costs $1

Magickal Childe, Inc.
35 West 19th Street
New York, NY 10011
(212) 242-7182
herbal oils; also has nonmainstream book selection with volumes on historic, mystical, and medicinal herbal usages

Meadowsweet Herb Farm
729 Eastham Road
Mount Holly Road
Shrewsbury, VT 05738
(802) 492-3565
potpourri and country herbal gifts, including wreaths, centerpieces, baskets, and tussie-mussies; also carries herbal vinegars, seasonings, and party gifts

Pam Montgomery
Green Terrestrial
Box 41, Route 9W
Milton, NY 12547
(914) 795-5238
wildcrafted and organically grown medicinal herbal preparations, including dandelion tinctures, yarrow tinctures, calendula oil, and mugwort dream pillows

Mother Tinctures
Dixon Road
Boulder, CO 80302
send SASE for information on tapes and reference manual instructing how to create medicinal herb salves, oils, and skin-care products

Nature's Way Products, Inc.
Dep't. H
Springville, UT 84663
organically grown medicinal herb products

Pegasus Products, Inc.
P.O. Box 228
Boulder, CO 80306
(303) 442-0319
(800) 577-6104
floral essences and homeopathic
combinations

Raven's Nest
4539 Iroquois Trail
Duluth, GA 30136
selection of herbal gifts, including
extracts, essential oils, and potpourri;
catalog costs $1

The Rosemary House
120 South Market Street
Mechanicsburg, PA 17055
(717) 697-5111
herbal crafts and scents; also carries
cooking oils and herbal culinary blends
and seeds

Shale Hill Farm
6856 Hommelville Road
Saugerties, NY 12477
retail farm shop sells herbal gifts and
crafts

SunFeather Herbal Soap Company
R.D. 3
Box 102
Potsdam, NY 13676
handmade herbally scented soaps and
bath accessories

Swissette Herb Farm
Clove Road
Salisbury Mills, NY 12577
retail farm shop sells herbal gifts,
potpourri, essential oils, and tinctures

Tom Thumb Workshop
Route 13
P.O. Box 357
Mappsville, VA 23407
potpourri ingredients and custom blends,
as well as apothecary jars and potpourri
bowls

Varney's Chemist Laden
Fredricksburg Herb Farm
310 East Main Street
Fredricksburg, TX 78624
(800) 284-0526
essential oils, herbal bath preparations,
sleep pillows, tussie-mussies

Westwood Studio Project
3020 South National
Box 123
Springfield, MO 65804
herbal coloring books, recipes and
notepads, calendars; catalog costs $1

Woodland Park Cottage Shop
6208 Phinney Avenue North
Seattle, WA 98103
retail store run by the Herbfarm (see
"Culinary Herbal Gifts") offers same
broad herbal product selection

Yield House
Dep't. 1000
North Conway, NH 03860
(800) 258-4720
cobalt blue storage jars (can be used for
dried herbal materials)

Herb Gardens to Visit

Please call ahead for hours; also consult
the guidebook *Traveler's Guide to Herb
Gardens,* published by the Herb Society
of America—see "Educational
Organizations and Individuals."

Abigail Adams Smith Museum
421 East 61st Street
New York, NY 10021
(212) 838-6878
historic house with herb garden

American Indian Archaeological Institute
Curtis Road
Washington, CT 06793
(203) 868-0518
wild native plants used for medicine,
dyes, and food

Arkansas Territorial Restoration
Third and Scott Streets
Little Rock, AZ 72201
"frontier pharmacy" medicinal garden
representing plants used by early settlers
in Arkansas

Bartram's House and Garden
54th & Lindbergh Boulevard
Philadelphia, PA 19143
(215) 729-5281
eighteenth-century herb garden

Berkshire Garden Center
Stockbridge, MA 02162
(413) 298-3926
garden with culinary and medicinal
herbs; also features daylilies and
wildflower meadow

Black Creek Pioneer Village
1000 Murray Ross Parkway,
Downsview, Ontario M3J 2P3
Canada
(416) 661-6610
carefully researched medicinal garden;
authentic nineteenth-century kitchen
garden; and representational dye garden
for weavers

Boscobel
Route 9-D
Garrison-on-Hudson, NY 10524
(914) 265-3638
herb and rose gardens

Boyce Thompson Southwestern
Arboretum
P.O. Box AB
Route 60/70
Superior, AZ 85273
(602) 689-2811
Southwestern desert plants, some with
herbal usages, as well as a designated
herb garden

Canterbury Shaker Village
288 Shaker Road
Canterbury, NH 03224
(603) 783-9511
Shaker museum with herb garden

Chicago Botanic Garden
P.O. Box 400
Lake Cook Road
Glencoe, IL 60022
(312) 835-5440
herb garden includes more than 200
species, arranged according to usages

The Cloisters
Metropolitan Museum of Art Medieval
Herb Garden at Bonnefont
Cloisters
Fort Tryon Park
New York, NY 10040
(212) 233-3700
Medieval-style herb garden

Colonial Williamsburg
Williamsburg, VA 23185
(804) 220-7645
living village museum with herb gardens

Cornell Plantations
The Robison York State Herb Garden
One Plantations Road
Ithaca, NY 14850
(607) 255-3020
one-acre reference collection of plants
important in botany, medicine, folklore,
and cottage industries

Denver Botanic Gardens
1005 York Street
Denver, CO 80206
(303) 331-4010
herb garden and rock garden
incorporating creeping thyme

Farmington Historic Home Museum
3033 Bardstown Road
Louisville, KY 40205
(502) 452 9920
nineteenth-century-style kitchen garden

Filoli
Cañada Road
Woodside, CA 94062
(415) 364-2880
knot garden and rose garden; old roses
also planted throughout grounds

Henry Ford Museum and Greenfield
Village
Oakwood Boulevard
Dearborn, MI 48121-1970
(313) 271-1620
lavender and general herb gardens

J. Paul Getty Museum
17985 Pacific Coast Highway
Malibu, CA 90265
(213) 458-2003
herbs known and cultivated in ancient
Greek and Roman times

Hancock Shaker Village
P.O. Box 898
Pittsfield, MA 01202
(413) 443-0188
Shaker herb garden, with same plants
grown for medicinal and seed industries

Inniswood Botanical Garden and Nature
Preserve
940 Hempstead Road
Westerville, OH 43081
(614) 895-6216
extensive thyme collection, including
thyme seats and lawns, as well as a
range of other herbs used for medicine,
cooking, and fragrance

Jenkins Estate Old Farmhouse
P.O. Box 5868
Southwest 209th and Farmington Road
(entrance at Grabhorn Road)
Aloha, OR 97006
(503) 642-3855
nineteenth-century farmhouse with
period herb "rustic" garden acting as
borders for raised beds and a log pergola
covered with pre-1912 roses; 50 varieties
of scented-leaf geraniums and
Chamomile

Living History Farms
2600 N.W. 111 Street
Des Moines, IA 50322
(515) 278-5286
period farms exemplifying different eras
of American life with a formal Victorian
herb garden and informal, pioneer-style
plantings

Los Angeles Arboretum
301 North Baldwin Avenue
Arcadia, CA 91007
(818) 446-8251
herbs divided by theme, color, and
function; Shakespeare, Shaker, Native,
and Mexican herb beds

Mission Mill Village and Museum
1313 Mill Street SE
Salem, OR 97301
(503) 585-7012
garden contains culinary, medicinal, and
dye herbs from mid-nineteenth century
labeled according to usage; woolen mill
with community of quilters and weavers
on premises

Morris-Jumel Mansion
W. 160th Street and Edgecombe Avenue
New York, NY 10032
(212) 923-8008
boxwood-and-rose garden at historic
home

Mount Vernon
The Mount Vernon Ladies' Association of
the Union
Mount Vernon, VA 22121
(703) 780-2000
formal kitchen garden with herbs

Nantucket Maria Mitchell Ass'n Herb
Garden
2 Vestal Street
Nantucket, MA 02554
508-228-0898
features eighteenth- and nineteenth-
century herbs grown for a variety of uses

The National Herb Garden
U.S. National Arboretum
3501 New York Avenue NE
Washington, DC 20002
specialty herb gardens arranged
according to usages

Ogden House
1520 Bronson Road
Fairfield, CT 06430
(203) 259-6356
eighteenth-century-style kitchen and
herb garden

Old Slater Mill Museum, Fiber and Dye
Garden
P.O. Box 727
Pawtucket, RI 02862
(401) 725-8638
small but interesting fiber and dye
garden

Old Sturbridge Village
Sturbridge, MA 01566
(508) 347-3362
living museum with herb garden; seeds,
crafts, gifts also available

Plimouth Plantation
Plymouth, MA 02360
(508) 746-1622
seventeenth-century-style village; kitchen
gardens with herbs

Rosedown
Highway 10 and Highway 61
St. Francisville, LA 70775
(504) 635-3332
herb garden at antebellum plantation
home

Santa Fe Trail Center
Route 3
Larned, KS 67550
(316) 285-2054
annual-and-perennial herb garden
surrounded by a walled courtyard in the
Spanish style

Shaker Museum
Old Chatham, NY 12316
(518) 794-9100
Shaker-style herb garden

Shakertown at Pleasant Hill
3500 Lexington Road
Harrodsburg, KY 40330
(606) 734-5411
medicinal Shaker herb garden

Shelburne Museum
Route 7
Shelburne, VT 05482
(802) 985-3344
garden with culinary, fragrance, and dye
herbs

Strawberry Banke
Court Street
Portsmouth, NH 03801
(603) 436-8032
decorative and medicinal herb garden

Tempe Wick House (at Jockey Hollow)
Morristown, NJ 07960
Colonial kitchen garden

Tucson Botanical Gardens
2150 North Alvernon Way
Tucson, AZ 85712
(602) 326-9255
general herb garden, as well as
collection of desert plants, many with
historic herbal usages

University of Minnesota Landscape
Arboretum
3675 Arboretum Drive
Chanhassen, MN 55317
(612) 443-2460
remarkable variety of herbs that can
withstand cold winters; knot and cloister
gardens

Western Reserve Herb Garden
Garden Center of Greater Cleveland
11030 East Boulevard in University Circle
Cleveland, OH 44106
(216) 721-1600
knot and theme gardens incorporating
numerous herb species

Educational Organizations and Individuals

Abundant Life Seed Foundation
P.O. Box 772
Port Townsend, WA 98368
(206) 385-5660
nonprofit organization dedicated to
acquiring, propagating, and preserving
plants and seeds of native and
naturalized flora, with emphasis on
species not commercially available; see
also "Herb Plants and Seeds"

California School of Herbal Studies
Box 39
Forestville, CA 95436
(707) 887-7457

Herb Research Foundation
P.O. Box 2602
Longmont, CO 80501
(303) 449-2265
provides information on medicinal herb
usages

The Herb Society of America
9019 Kirtland Chardon Road
Mentor, OH 44060
(216) 256-0514
publishes valuable guidebook entitled
*Traveler's Guide to Herb Gardens: Over
500 Gardens in the United States and
Canada Featuring Herbs*

Heritage Seed Program/
Canadian Organic Growers
RR3
Uxbridge, Ontario
LOC 1KO
Canada
project dedicated to acquiring and
preserving heirloom and endangered
food crops; membership open to anyone;
members receive periodical three times
per year

International Herb Growers and
Marketers Association
P.O. Box 281
Silver Springs, PA 17575
(717) 684-9756
publishes *Herb Grower and Marketer,* a
bimonthly newsletter; members can
attend seminars and workshops

Jeanne Rose
219 Carl Street
San Francisco, CA 94117
offers herbal studies correspondence
course

Susun Weed
P.O. Box 64
Woodstock, NY 12498
(914) 246-8081
workshops and apprenticeships in herbal
medicine and spirit healing

BIBLIOGRAPHY

Antique Herbals and Herb Writings

Culpeper, Nicholas. *Culpeper's Complete Herbal.* Secaucus, N.J.: Chartwell Books, 1985. (Original edition, 1653; reprinted, London: Foulsham and Co., Ltd., n.d.)

Gerard, John. *The Herball or General Historie of Plantes.* Gathered by John Gerarde of London, Master in Chirurgerie, Very much Enlarged and Amended by Thomas Johnson, citizen and Apothecarye of London. New York: Dover Publications, 1975. (Original edition, London: Adam, Issip Joice Norton and Richard Whitakers, 1633.)

Monardes, Nicholas. *Joyfull Newes Out of the New-Found World.* Englished by John Frampton Marchant. New York: Alfred A. Knopf, 1925. (Original edition, London: Bonham Norton, 1596.)

Parkinson, John. *Paridisi in Sole Paradisus Terrestris.* New York: Dover Publications, 1975. (Original edition printed 1629; reprinted, London: Methuen and Company, 1904.)

Culinary Applications

Berglund, Berndt, and Clare E. Bolsby. *The Edible Wild: A Complete Cookbook and Guide to Edible Wild Plants in Canada and North America.* New York: Charles Scribner's Sons, 1971.

Flower, Barbara, and Elisabeth Rosenbaum. *The Roman Cookery Book of Apicius.* London: Peter Nevill, 1957.

Phillips, Robert. *Wild Food.* New York: Little, Brown and Co., Inc., 1986.

Root, Waverley. *Food: An Authoritative Visual History and Dictionary of the Foods of the World.* New York: Simon & Schuster, 1980.

Design and Cultivation

Bremness, Lesley. *The Complete Book of Herbs: A Practical Guide to Growing & Using Herbs.* New York: Viking Penguin, 1988.

Coats, Peter. *Roses.* London: Octopus Books Ltd., 1962.

Christopher, Thomas. *In Search of Lost Roses.* New York: Summit Books, 1989.

Gessert, Kate Rogers. Illustrations by George Gessert, Jr. *The Beautiful Food Garden: Creative Landscaping with Vegetables, Herbs, Fruits, & Flowers.* Pownal, Vt.: Storey Communications, 1987.

Jabs, Carolyn. *The Heirloom Gardener.* San Francisco: Sierra Club Books, 1984.

Kourik, Robert. Foreword by Rosalind Creasy. *Designing and Maintaining Your Edible Landscape Naturally.* Santa Rosa, Calif.: Metamorphic Press, 1986.

Reid, Shirley. *Herbs for the Home and Garden.* London: Angus & Robertson Publishers, 1985.

Swindells, Philip. *The Harlow Car Book of Herb Gardening.* North Pomfret, Vt.: David & Charles Inc., 1987.

Foraging and Identification

Berglund, Berndt, and Clare E. Bolsby. (See "Culinary Applications.")

Brimble, L. H. F. *Flowers in Britain.* London: Macmillan and Co., 1944.

Gibbons, Euell. *Stalking the Wild Asparagus.* New York: David McKay Co., Inc., 1970.

Hedrick, U. P. *Sturtevant's Edible Plants of the World.* New York: Dover Publications, 1972.

Knutsen, Karl. *Wild Plants You Can Eat: A Guide to Identification and Preparation.* Garden City, N.Y.: Doubleday & Co., 1975.

Millspaugh, Charles F. (See "Household and Medicinal Applications.")

Peterson, Lee. *A Field Guide to Edible Wild Plants of Eastern and Central North America.* Boston: Houghton Mifflin, 1977.

Peterson, Roger Tory, and Margaret McKenny. *A Field Guide to Wildflowers of Northeastern and North-central North America.* Boston: Houghton Mifflin, 1968.

Tutin, T. G., et al. *Flora Europea.* vol 2. Cambridge: Cambridge University Press, 1968.

Folklore and Mysticism

Calvino, Italo. *Italian Folktales.* Translated by George Martin. New York: Harcourt Brace Jovanovich, 1980.

Cavendish, Richard. *The Black Arts.* New York: G. P. Putnam's Sons, 1967.

Coats, Alice M. *Flowers and Their Histories.* New York: Pitman Publishing Corporation, 1906.

D'Andrea, Jeanne. Illustrations by Martha Breen Bredemeyer. *Ancient Herbs.* Malibu, Calif.: The J. Paul Getty Museum, 1982.

Frazer, Sir James George. *The Golden Bough: A Study in Magic and Religion.* 3rd ed., part VII, vol. 2. New York: St. Martin's Press, 1966.

Friend, Hilderic. *Flower Lore.* Rockport, Mass.: Para Research, 1981.

Jacob, Dorothy. *A Witch's Guide to Gardening.* Foreword by B. J. Chute. New York: Taplinger Publishing Co., Inc., 1964.

Robbins, Rossell Hope. *The Encyclopedia of Witchcraft and Demonology.* New York: Crown, 1959.

Thorndike, Lynn. *History of Magic & Experimental Sciences.* vols. 1–8. New York: Columbia University Press, 1941.

Weston, Jessie L. *From Ritual to Romance.* Garden City, N.Y.: Doubleday, 1964.

Gardening and Related History

Coats, Alice M. *The Plant Hunters.* New York: McGraw Hill, 1969.

DeForest, Elizabeth K. *The Gardens and Grounds at Mount Vernon.* Mount Vernon, Va.: The Ladies' Association of the Union, 1982.

Favretti, Rudy J. and Joy. *For Every House a Garden: A Guide for Reproducing Period Gardens.* Chester, Conn.: The Pequot Press, 1977.

Fay, Peter W. *The Opium War, 1840–1842.* New York: W. W. Norton & Co., 1976.

Gabel, Creighton, ed. *Man Before History.* Englewood Cliffs, N.J.: Prentice-Hall, 1964.

Heiser, Charles B. *The Sunflower.* Norman, Okla.: Univ. of Oklahoma Press, 1981.

Horgan, Edward R. *The Shaker Holy Land: A Community Portrait.* Foreword by Faith Andrews. Introduction by Robert F. W. Meade. Harvard, Mass.: The Harvard Common Press, 1982.

Huxley, Anthony. *An Illustrated History of Gardening.* New York and London: Paddington Press, 1978.

Leighton, Ann. *Early American Gardens: 'For Meate or Medicine.'* Boston: Houghton Mifflin, 1970.

Miller, Amy Bess. *Shaker Herbs: A History and Compendium.* New York: Clarkson N. Potter, 1976.

Robinson, William. Introduction by Robin Lane Fox. *The Wild Garden.* London: The Scolar Press, 1977.

Household and Medicinal Applications

Lust, John L. *The Herb Book.* New York: Bantam, 1974.

Meyer, Joseph E. *The Herbalist.* Printed by author, 1918. Reprinted by Clarence Meyer, 1973.

Millspaugh, Charles F. *American Medicinal Plants: An Illustrated and Descriptive Guide to Plants Indigenous to and Naturalized in the United States Which Are Used in Medicine.* New York: Dover Publications, 1974.

Reid, Daniel P. *Chinese Herbal Medicine.* Wellinborough, N.H.: Thorsons Publishing Group, 1987.